CW00829433

Beverley

by

K. A. MacMahon

Edited by John Markham

Illustrations by Patricia E. Deans

Highgate of Beverley

Highgate Publications (Beverley) Limited
2004

British Library Cataloguing in Publication Data.
A catalogue record for this book is available from the British Library.

© Highgate Publications (Beverley) Limited 2004

ISBN 1 902645 40 5

Published by

Highgate of Beverley

Highgate Publications (Beverley) Limited
4 Newbegin, Beverley, HU17 8EG. Telephone (01482) 886017

Printed by Highgate Print Limited
4 Newbegin, Beverley, HU17 8EG. Telephone (01482) 886017

CONTENTS

Cover Pictures
Front: Beverley Minster towers
Back: The Court Room, Beverley Guildhall

Abbreviations used in footnotes:

Pevsner: see Pevsner, Nikolaus.
VCH: see *A History of the County of York.*
Both in Select Bibliography.

PREFACE
by John Markham

When Kenneth A. MacMahon died in 1972 at the age of 58. He had written only two chapters of his planned history of Hull. Fortunately his history of Beverley had been completed but (without the opportunity of a final reading of the printed text) it now became a posthumous publication.

The book was produced to commemorate the 400th anniversary of the granting of Beverley's charter of 1573, its aim to show the evolution of the town and its churches, the development of its character and appearance, and the continuity of events which linked past to present. It was a labour of love. Ken MacMahon was zealous for people to understand and appreciate their inheritance and in his short book he explained, in a concise, easily accessible account, how Beverley had become the town it was in the 1970s.

Many were inspired by his lectures to pursue a deeper study of aspects of history which they found of particular interest. In the three decades since Ken MacMahon's death, their work and that of many other historians and archaeologists have added considerably to the knowledge available on Beverley's history and to its fuller understanding. But the value of his book remains unchallenged as the best short introduction to the history of the town. More detail and fuller discussion can be obtained elsewhere, but this is a book by a writer who could see the whole picture and from his impressive scholarship could trace a clear route through the complexity of facts, figures, personalities and events to produce a readable account which brought a vast subject within the grasp of a wide readership.

A relatively small number of minor amendments have been made to the text of the original edition. I am extremely grateful to Arthur Credland, Professor Barbara English and the ever-helpful staff of the Beverley Reference Library for their generous assistance in this editorial task. Equally, I am delighted that Patricia E. Deans has supplied illustrations from her excellent collection to enhance the text. Once again I thank Ian and Margaret Sumner for their excellent proof-reading and indexing services.

The massive expansion of local historical studies in the years since Ken MacMahon's death has resulted in a plethora of publications. A short bibliography of works has been selected from those published in this period as a guide to those who wish to read further. The absence of any title is in no way to be interpreted as criticism. Many more are equally worthy of inclusion.

FOREWORD
to the original edition by K. A. MacMahon

Within the imposed limits of too few pages the attempt has here been made to survey thirteen hundred years of Beverley's history. Of necessity much has had to be omitted and more glossed over where the pen would willingly have lingered longer. But – to paraphrase the words of an ancient writer – while it is the business of the good huntsman in the wood to take what he can, it cannot be held to his charge that he did not take all. Probably this may be allowed to excuse the many shortcomings of the brief historical sketch which follows.

But historians of all breeds are invariably under obligation to others, and despite his foraging in wider-ranging archives the present writer would acknowledge in particular his appreciation to the Mayor, Corporation and Town Clerk of Beverley, the East Riding County Archivist, the Librarian of the Brynmor Jones Library of the University of Hull, the Chief Librarian of the Kingston-upon-Hull City Libraries and their respective staffs for many kindnesses in making records and materials available. Nor can he be unmindful of personal indebtedness to the many friends and fellow students both young and old with whom Beverley's story has been discussed in University Seminar and Extra-Mural class alike. But they can all enjoy the relief of an 'escape' clause; the author alone accepts responsibility for every sin of omission and commission herein.

An Appreciation of K. A. MacMahon

K. A. MacMahon was a scholar and historian of repute. Senior Lecturer in the History Department at Hull University, he was also a Fellow of the Royal Historical Society and a Fellow of the Society of Antiquaries. He served as an examiner at Keele and Strathclyde Universities. He was an acknowledged leading authority in his own field of study – the history of Beverley and the East Riding. This reputation was not lightly earned but was the result of a lifetime's patient research.

His literary output may not be considered prodigious by some standards but was, in fact, limited by two major factors. In the first place, that everything he wrote was judged by his own high standards and was scrupulously accurate, and secondly that, as he saw it, his students and teaching were very much his firm duty, research and writing an absorbing hobby. Not for him the comparatively easy way of climbing to fame on the backs of his students. But K. A. MacMahon did achieve fame in the regard and respect of thousands of East Riding people, ordinary people who often, for the first time, came to a realization of the significance of the architectural treasures about us, of the development of our democratic forms of government, of the patterns of our roads and the growth of our trade and commerce. To them Ken MacMahon was the fount of knowledge, a lecturer with a heart, with the patience and kindness and humanity that are not always concomitant with scholarship and learning.

Eric Bielby

1. BEFORE THE NORMANS

In times past some of the older school of antiquarians have attempted to accord the capital of the East Riding an origin dating back to Roman times. Unfortunately, the evidence is completely lacking and the theory that the town was the Petuaria of the Parisii* was effectively demolished in 1939 when archaeological discovery proved that the claim of Brough-on-Humber to be Romano-British Petuaria was wholly justified. Beverley grew up with its Minster and it is doubtful if anything akin to a settlement worthy of notice existed much before the middle years of the 10th century.

The philologists are in broad agreement that the first element in the modern name form, Beverley, is the Old English (OE) 'beofor' (beaver), an animal long extinct in this country but one which was once native to England. The derivation of the second element, 'ley', is more debatable. Some years ago, Professor E. V. Gordon suggested that the name as a whole may be possibly derived from a British (i.e. Celtic) name form such as 'bebrolicos', giving the meaning 'beaver stream'. Other scholars such as Eilert Ekwall have favoured a combination of 'beofor' and some unrecorded OE word 'licc', also giving the meaning 'beaver stream'. Probably more acceptable than either theory is the one that the name is compounded of OE 'beofor' and OE 'leah', the latter word originally denoting woodland but with a later sense of 'clearing in woodland'. Debate

on the subject is but an academic exercise but the majority of scholars today would probably now favour the 'beofor-leah' theory, i.e. the 'beaver clearing in woodland'.

The history of early Beverley is indissolubly linked with that of its

Archaeological investigation in Wylies Road of the town ditch, 1985.

* Romano-British earthworks have been identified on the Westwood. In 1985 an excavation in Wylies Road revealed a Romano-British ditch as well as 3rd- and 4th-century pottery.

famous Minster church and begins with John, fourth bishop of York after Paulinus.

In his great work, *The Ecclesiastical History of the English People*, completed in 731, Bede, the scholar-monk of Jarrow and Monkwearmouth, recorded for posterity something of the life and times of John, Bishop of Hexham, who in 705 was translated to the see of York. It may be noted here that the bishop of York was not raised to the status and dignity of archbishop until 735. When advancing years compelled the laying aside of episcopal cares John retired in 718 to his own monastery of Inderauuda (i.e. 'in the wood of the men of Deira'): there on 7 May 721 he died and was buried in the *porticus* or sidechapel of St Peter in the monastic church. Bede's biographical sketch of John is partly explained by a personal interest in the bishop for it was at Bishop John's hands that Bede was ordained deacon at the early age of 19 and priested at 30. It was understandable, therefore, that the Northumbrian scholar-monk should hold Bishop John in special and kindly remembrance.

The monastery of Inderauuda was probably founded by Bishop John soon after his translation to York in 705. As Bede makes clear, the Bishop went into retreat whenever opportunity offered and especially so in time of Lent: in the monastery in the Deiran woodlands he would find the prayerful seclusion he sought, just as, when Bishop of Hexham, he had periodically retired to an isolated spot north of the Tyne probably now represented by St John Lee.

Bede gives further biographical details about John who, he says, was one of the five bishops of the early church in Northumbria who were nurtured in the Abbess Hilda's famous monastery at Streoneshalh (Whitby). Partly on the authority of Berthun, formerly John's deacon, 'a most reverend and truthful man', Bede records details of miracles of healing by the Bishop and recounts another miracle on the testimony of Herebald, then Abbot of Tynemouth. In his survey Bede provides the interesting information that the Bishop dedicated the churches of two thegns, Puch and Addi, whose estates were not too distant from the monastery: later tradition has sought to identify these churches with Bishop Burton and Cherry Burton respectively. The nunnery at Wetadun (normally identified as Watton, north of Beverley) was the scene of another of John's miracles, and the later (1150) foundation of a house of Gilbertine nuns there could represent, as in the case of Reinfrid's re-foundation of Whitby (c.1078), a deliberate reintroduction of monastic life on the acknowledged site of an earlier monastery.

Nothing historically is known of Bishop John's monastery after his death. Speculation on its character and layout must be measured by what is known from excavations at Whitby and elsewhere and from the known character of Irish Celtic monasteries as evidenced at Monasterboice (Co. Louth) and Clonmacnoise (Co. Offaly). The monastery of Inderauuda was probably little else than a collection of crudely built wooden oratoria or

The frithstool, associated with the granting of sanctuary, but may have been the episcopal throne of St. John of Beverley.

Tomb of St John of Beverley.

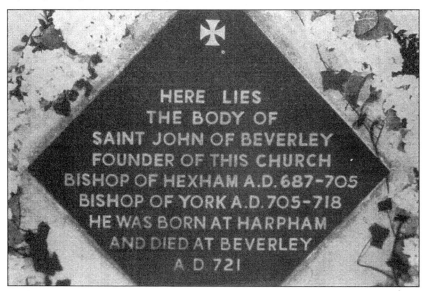

HERE LIES
THE BODY OF
SAINT JOHN OF BEVERLEY
FOUNDER OF THIS CHURCH
BISHOP OF HEXHAM A.D. 687-705
BISHOP OF YORK A.D. 705-718
HE WAS BORN AT HARPHAM
AND DIED AT BEVERLEY
A.D. 721

cells with possibly a refectory, all set in unplanned and somewhat disorganised fashion round a small monastic church and within a boundary marked by stream, ditch or bank. Strange though it may seem, it is not even possible to prove that the present great Minster church of Beverley occupied the site of this early monastery, although, of course, the circumstantial evidence is strong: only a massive, painstaking and highly scientific excavation of the Minster site and its immediate environs could possibly provide the necessary proof. Nevertheless, the plain stone chair, the so-called *frithstol*, which occupies an honoured place in the sanctuary of the Minster, could well date from the days of John's monastery.

At this early stage in history it is only possible to surmise that a small community of traders might tend to develop in the vicinity of the monastery, if only because of the growing fame of the relics of Bishop John who, as Bede made clear, had a reputation in his lifetime as a healer of the sick and the dumb. But, even if the monastic community had survived natural disasters such as fire and plague, it is a tolerable certainty that by the middle years of the 9th century it would have been wiped out or dispersed as a result of Danish raiding. Such a view does not, however, rule out the possibility of a speedy rehabilitation of the monastic community when circumstances changed even temporarily for the better. According to the *Anglo-Saxon Chronicle* the 'heathen men' attacked God's church in Lindisfarne in 793 and thereafter the scale of Danish attacks on this country increased in frequency and strength. It is highly unlikely that monasteries such as Inderauuda, Wetadun and Lastingham survived intact the establishment of the Viking kingdom of York in 867. But the memory of the holy Bishop John remained and years of dearth, devastation and misery would merely serve to enhance and embellish the reputation of one to whom seemingly miraculous powers of healing had been divinely vouchsafed.

When the worst of the Viking onslaught was over, it is very likely that some form of religious community life began anew on the site of John's monastery. Certainly by the time of King Athelstan (924-39) a community of clergy was in being and the wonder-working relics of John, which were in their care, had apparently acquired considerable reputation. On his way north in 934 to demonstrate the military might of the House of Wessex and possibly in retaliation for an unfriendly act by the King of the Scots, Athelstan was induced to turn aside and in prayer at the bishop's tomb seek the intercessory help of the yet uncanonised John. According to the dramatic story related by William Ketell over 150 years later, Athelstan left his army on the way north and with a few companions visited the tomb of the holy John. There the King 'poured out hearty prayers' and, to use Ketell's colourful language, 'drenched the pavement with his tears' in supplicating the aid of the long-dead bishop. Athelstan left his dagger on the altar in pledge that he would return to redeem it at a good price if he were successful in the expected forthcoming struggle – a bargain with the

Almighty which only makes sense in a medieval context. The King of the Scots did not offer battle on this occasion but, three years later (937), an alliance of the Norse leader Olaf of Dublin and the Kings of Scotland and Strathclyde was overwhelmingly defeated by Athelstan and his brother Edmund at Brunanburh – a battle site which has yet to be identified.

The royal visit and the memorable military achievement of the House of Wessex had striking results for the church at Beverley. Athelstan redeemed his promise, endowed the church with lands and privileges, including a 'tithe' of four thraves* from every plough in the East Riding and special rights of sanctuary; and he refounded the existing establishment as a secular collegiate church, i.e. served by secular canons and not by 'regular' religious. It is to these churches, usually of royal or episcopal foundation, served by such secular canons (York, Lincoln and Southwell are typical examples) that the term Minster (OE *mynstir*) has clung. The historical significance of these events in the early history of Beverley and its great church also lies in the fact that throughout the medieval period it was King Athelstan, and not Bishop John, who was regarded as the founder of the Minster church. This refoundation and grant of royal privileges can therefore be dated within narrow limits to between 934 and the King's death in 939.

The charter by which Athelstan granted these privileges and rights has

---

* 1 thrave = 4 sheaves; 4 sheaves = 316 lb (143 kg).

17th-century painting of King Athelstan and St John.

not survived and the so-called rhyming charter of Athelstan which begins:

> 'This know all men, whoever they may be
> Who hear and see this charter . . .'

is an early 14th-century compilation, the original of which is among the Cottonian collection of charters in the British Museum. Unfortunately, this charter of the first 'King of all Britain' which so fortuitously appeared in the period when the first two Edwards were trying to establish their claim to the Scottish crown, is demonstrably spurious. Quite apart from other diplomatic and historical considerations, the notification:

> 'That I the Kinge Adelstan
> Has yaten (granted) and giuen to Sente Johan
> Of Beverlik . . .'

unwittingly endows Athelstan with an unusual degree of foresight for Bishop John was not canonised until almost a century after the death of Athelstan.

The royal refoundation (with all that it implied in terms of fame and prestige), plus the substantial royal grant of lands and privileges, meant that a community of traders would tend to grow up in close association with the Minster church. The Danish onslaught of England had wrought unspeakable havoc but it must not be overlooked that the Scandinavian peoples were traders and colonists as well as warriors and sailors. The infusion of Viking blood into the racial stock of northern England had important long-term economic results and led to the stimulation of town life: not least of all was the stimulus given to trading contracts with northern Europe. The economic vitality and relative prosperity of York c.1000, for example, is interestingly attested by the biographer of Archbishop Oswald (972-92) who commented at the time he was writing that the city was 'filled with the treasures of merchants, chiefly of Danish race, who had come to York from every quarter'. With its important Minster church, the shrine of its saintly bishop attracting the pilgrim, a favourable geographical position and navigable waterway links with the broad estuary of the Humber, it is difficult to believe that Beverley did not in some degree share York's commercial fortune. As in many another Yorkshire town, the Scandinavian impact of a thousand years ago had its own memorial in Beverley's street names: Eastgate, Flemingate, Walkergate, Keldgate, Lairgate, Highgate, Minstermoorgate and Hengate, although of course not necessarily pre- or immediately post-Conquest in origin and name, have as their final element the English form of the Old Norse *gata* (road, street). Figham, one of Beverley's pastures, should more correctly be Faegang (cattle track), a common Danish term and one often found in Danish place names.

In the half century before the Norman conquest, Beverley's Minster, like the great churches of Southwell and Ripon, was splendidly endowed and beautified by the last three Saxon archbishops of York, Aelfric Puttoc, Cynesige and Ealdred. It was in the archiepiscopate of Puttoc (1023-51) that the growing cult of John came to a fitting climax with the canonisation in 1037 of the holy Bishop as St John of Beverley. A shrine of gold, silver and precious stones was made at this time for his relics. A greater emphasis on community life of the clergy at Beverley is indicated by the fact that Puttoc began the building of a refectory and dormitory. During his period as archbishop the church was additionally endowed by grants and properties and also apparently by substantial gifts from a certain, but otherwise historically unknown, Forceus.

Archbishop Puttoc's successor, Cynesige (1051-60), continued the dormitory and refectory building projects, provided the church with books and adorned it in a variety of other ways. But Cynesige will be particularly remembered in the Minster's history for his special building contribution of a magnificent stone tower: it was the fall of this tower in the early years of the 13th century, under circumstances which will be described in due course, which occasioned the building of the present fabric.

The influence of Ealdred, the last of the pre-Conquest archbishops (1062-69), was in some ways even more significant than that of his two immediate predecessors. A monk of Winchester and later Abbot of Tavistock and high in favour with Edward the Confessor, Ealdred became archbishop in 1062 and had the dubious honour of crowning William in 1066 and Matilda in 1068. He seems to have established and regularised his position as Lord of Beverley by procuring a writ of notification from Edward, addressed to Earl Tostig and the thegns in Yorkshire, that the Archbishop of York was the sole Lord of Beverley and that at Beverley there should be 'the minster life and assembly while that any man lives'. He completed the dormitory and refectory building schemes and enlarged the pre-Conquest church by building a new presbytery. This we are told 'he dedicated in honour of St John the Evangelist' – an interesting point in itself inasmuch as the medieval dedication of the church was in honour of St John the Evangelist and not, as is so often mistakenly stated, in honour of St John of Beverley. Ealdred also decorated the Minster with paintings and adorned it with furnishings although the details are unspecified. A reference to a painted ceiling suggests the existence of a vault and, like the contemporary one in the Chapel of the Pyx at Westminster, this was doubtless 'Norman' in character at this point of time and was probably over the new presbytery.

The archbishop additionally gifted to the church a magnificent pulpitum of gold, silver and brass together with a rood of German smith work: iron work of comparable date can be seen today in the Domkirche at Hildesheim in Lower Saxony. This particular gift doubtless reflected Ealdred's own connections with Germany for in 1054, and prior to his becoming archbishop, he had been Edward's ambassador to the court of the

Emperor Henry III at Cologne. On matters of church organisation and discipline he may well have been influenced by Archbishop Herman of Cologne and other contemporaries for he is credited with unspecified modification of the 'minster life' at Beverley during his archiepiscopate. It is very probable that such 'modification' was an increased emphasis on the corporate life. It was reputedly at Ealdred's request, and doubtless designed to help to emphasise the importance of the see of York vis-à-vis that of Canterbury, that Folcard, a monk of St Bertin in Flanders and later abbot of Thorney (Cambs.), wrote a 'Life' of St John of Beverley. As was characteristic medieval practice in such circumstances, Folcard did not hesitate to incorporate in his work tradition as historical fact and as a result the simple account of Bishop John given by Bede is considerably inflated at Folcard's hand. But the real significance of Folcard's essay in hagiography is that by the time of the Norman Conquest the cult of St John of Beverley, especially in the north, was both intense and widespread.

Thus, by the time of the death of Edward the Confessor in 1066, there was at Beverley a Minster church of some size and importance which, with Ripon and Southwell, was in a very real sense a sub-cathedral of the diocese of York. And, what is just as significant historically, is that in the vicinity of that church and on the lands of the archbishop of York, there is little doubt that a community of merchants and traders had already begun to develop.

Archbishop Thurstan's Charter c.1129.

2. MEDIEVAL TOWN AND BOROUGH

The trading community which in due course grew up at the gates of the early Minster church enjoyed certain obvious economic and geographical advantages. Access to Beverley was relatively easy, and the fact that today seven major roads converge on the town reflects the existence of various routes and trackways which in early days had led to the church and shrine of the Blessed John. Such good communications stimulated the growth of trade, market and fair alike, and the town's early regional economic dominance was maintained until it began to be seriously challenged by Hull in the 14th century.

The site of the town in a well-watered countryside and on the lower eastern slopes of wold conditioned its topographical character. Streams from the higher land flowed down into the valley of the River Hull, and the natural wind of these watercourses helped to determine the serpentine character of Beverley's early streets. In a well-wooded countryside evaporation was minimal and hence run-off far greater than is the case today. Even as late as the end of the 17th century a writer could comment on the 'pleasant springs' running through Beverley's streets. Progressively these town watercourses were culverted and street levels raised, but well after 1800 sections of the important Walker Beck, for example, which flowed along the west side of Walkergate, and from thence to the west of the Minster, were still open. The build-up of the town along the lines of these streams produced an excessively elongated rather than a nucleated town plan.

The three-quarters of a mile of canalised natural waterway known as Beverley Beck was also a factor making for economic growth. The Beck, tidal until the lock was built in 1802, gave access to the Humber by way of the River Hull and therefore, in days when sea-going vessels were no bigger than the modern river barge, the town enjoyed the status and the advantages of a river port. Understandably, there was concern to ensure that the navigation of the Beck was maintained.

Trading activities came more and more to the fore after the Norman Conquest and c.1121-22 Henry I granted to Archbishop Thurstan as the Lord of Beverley, and to the canons of the Minster, the right to increase the annual fair in the town from two days to five with 'protection' for all persons coming to buy and sell. These years marked a significant stage in evolution to borough status for, at about this time, and certainly not later than 1129 (which is its effective downward date), Thurstan granted a charter to the men of Beverley according them the liberties of the men of York, the privilege of having their own 'hanshus' ('where they might deliberate their laws') and, on payment of 18 marks per annum, the right to all toll except on the three designated feasts of St John of Beverley, the Translation of St John and the Nativity of St John the Baptist. Even then the burgesses themselves were to be free of toll and they were also to be toll-free throughout Yorkshire. The original charter, one of the oldest town charters extant, is preserved at the East Riding of Yorkshire Archives Services. Its provisions were confirmed by Henry I soon after its issue and the men of Beverley were additionally granted rights of free burgage. Charters, confirmatory and others, followed from king and archbishop, including a confirmation charter issued at Worms by Richard I during his captivity in Germany – some indication of the fact that the men of Beverley helped to ransom the royal crusader, as charters had to be paid for, and the Crown was well aware that, collectively, chartered rights and privileges were a marketable commodity. King John's state of chronic penury resulted in the borough acquiring from the Crown the important additional privilege of freedom from toll 'throughout all our land', except in the City of London, plus a second charter of royal confirmation of earlier grants (1199). These two charters cost the burgesses the immense sum of £333. 6s. 8d. (500 marks). Understandably payment was 'by instalment', but the ability of the Beverley merchant community by this time to meet such charter 'costage' is in itself indicative both of economic growth and of due appreciation of the value of chartered privileges.

Wool export, cloth manufacture and, to a lesser extent, tanning, developed as the town's basic economic activities, and varied medieval records attested such development. By the reign of Henry III, Beverley cloths had acquired a considerable reputation and in 1236, for example, the King ordered merchants of the town, who were attending Stowe Fair, to provide certain high quality cloths for royal use: payment for these was promised at London the following Michaelmas. Beverley merchants also grew wealthy as exporters of wool and there is more than mere indication of this. In 1306, for example, Wynand Morant complained to the Crown that certain merchants of Groningen, despite repeated demands for settlement, were indebted to him to the extent of £272 and were refusing payment. The Crown made a series of requests to the Bishop of Utrecht that right should be done by Wynand, but without effect, and in 1309, as was usual in such cases, the Sheriff of Yorkshire was ordered to seize goods of Groningen merchants of appropriate value to ensure recompense to Wynand. Again, in 1313, William de Warter, John de Lund, Walter de Kelsterne and 13 other merchants of the town complained that they had hired three Flemish ships in Hull to export some £4,000 worth of wool, wool-fells and other merchandise to Flanders but that the vessels had been captured off the Scheldt and taken to Aberdeen. Apparently at Aberdeen the goods were 'delivered to other Flemings who were there with the King's enemies and by whom they were afterwards taken to Flanders'.

Such complaints naturally reflected the current state of Anglo-Flemish relations and in this particular case, after abortive diplomatic overtures to the Count of Flanders, orders were issued for the arrest of Flemings' goods in various east coast ports between London and Newcastle to ensure these Beverley merchants were reimbursed. These are but two examples and it is clear that by the 14th century many Beverley merchants were prospering. In 1326 a merchant like Thomas de Holme of Beverley was able to advance £300 to the Prior of Sempringham in Lincolnshire – presumably an advance on the monastic wool clip: nine years later, in 1335, William, the Prior of Malton (another house of the order of Sempringham), formally acknowledged his convent's indebtedness to Thomas de Holme for nearly £1,000 for wool to be supplied against cash already advanced. And, on the eve of war with France, many Beverley merchants (John de Thornton, William de Copendale, William de Kelsterne, Walter Frost and Thomas de Holme among them) were in a position to make substantial loans in the Crown in 1337. None of these merchants was in the Hull de la Pole class but they were obviously men of substance.

Despite war, pestilence and national economic growing pains, it would be true to say that the town reached the height of its medieval economic prosperity and importance by the second half of the 14th century: thereafter, a gradual decline set in as both York and Beverley were progressively overhauled as textile manufacturing centres by the up-and-coming clothing towns of the West Riding. But in 1377 Beverley was a sizeable town and on the evidence of the poll tax returns of that year may well have had a population of 5,000, which was about half that of York and more than twice that of Hull. Town life was vigorous and the variety of trades in the town is illustrated by the number of gilds, the records of which largely exist in the form of ordinances registered in 14th- and 15th-century borough records. In 1390, for instance, no fewer than 38 gilds, ranging from skinners to goldsmiths and merchants to mariners, were named as having responsibility for the production of the Corpus Christi plays that year. Their identification with the parish churches through the maintenance of lights at various altars was particularly close. Each gild organised its trading activities, fixed prices within limits, tried to enforce good standards of workmanship, made provision for the sick, needy and elderly of its members and, at the last, ensured them a seemly and decent funeral.

The gilds were closely supervised by the town's 'keepers', and gild ordinances had to be approved and registered. The butchers, for example, were not to wash the offal of their beasts in Walker Beck nor cast blood, horns, bones and guts in the street, nor privily pile it all up at the bar of the town – a traditional place for getting rid of filth and rubbish. A tanner who reproved the aldermen of his gild 'with unhonest or unseemly words' – a pale comprehensive description of what an honest Beverley tanner would be capable of when roused to anger – forfeited the fine of 3s. 4d. – of which the town took half. Somewhat understandably, the bakers were not to employ Scotsmen except under certain conditions, and no saddler was to work any tanned leather into reins, otherwise a demarcation dispute could follow because this activity came within the purview of the lorimers. Additional to merchant and craft gilds, there were religious and parish gilds such as those of Corpus Christi, the Blessed Mary, St Elen, Pasternoster and St John the Baptist.

As at York, by the end of the reign of Edward III , the Beverley gilds had become responsible, under civic control, for the organisation at Corpus Christi-tide of a play cycle of secularised versions of liturgical drama. Production of the plays cannot have been a regular annual event for both political circumstance and the incidence of plague would naturally lead to cancellation of plans. A gild, either singly or in concert with another gild, prepared and produced a play on a *pagina* or moveable stage. Each play was performed at seven different points in the town and any Beverlonian who was prepared to stand at one station throughout the day could see the whole Beverley play cycle from *The Fall of Lucifer* (the responsibility of the tilers) to *The Harrowing of Hell* and *Domesday*. There was dramatic appropriateness of gild choice or allocation of play: it was understandable that the watermen should produce *Noah's Ship*, the goldsmiths the play of the *Three Kings* and the cooks (with their experience of stoking up fires) the *Harrowing of Hell*. Unfortunately, unlike those of York and Chester, no text of the Beverley plays has survived.

The 'Governors' of the town kept a close supervisory control over the plays, towards the production of which the rank-and-file gildsman had to pay his 'pageant pence'. If a play failed to meet acceptable standards retribution followed: in 1520 Richard Trollope, the alderman of the painters' gild, was fined two shillings because his gild's play had been badly and confusedly played 'in contempt of the whole community and before many strangers', and in 1452 Henry Cowper, a weaver, was penalised because apparently he had not taken the trouble even to learn his lines. If a gild failed to produce its play a fine of 40 shillings might be imposed – a heavy penalty by the standards of the time. Civic pride, of course, was involved in all this. Very occasionally, there might be a hint of the 'props' required. In 1391, for instance, the Keepers handed over to John of Arras of the gild of Hairers (under penalty of 10 shillings for every default in their play called *Paradise* and one of 20 shillings for non-return of 'props') 'all necessaries . . . belonging to the said play': these were one 'Karre' (i.e. a *pagina*), eight hasps, eighteen staples, two visors, two angels' wings, one fir pole, one serpent, two pairs of linen boots, two pairs of shirts and a sword.

Changes in the pattern and organisation of the plays naturally occurred and the development of the 'morality' play is well evidenced in Beverley in the middle years of the 15th century. In 1467, for example, 39 of the town's gilds were responsible for a *Pater Noster* 'morality' play cycle performed on eight *paginae*. There was 'drama', too, in festival processions: the shrine of St John was carried round the town at Rogationtide and there is record that in 1389 on the Feast of the Blessed Virgin Mary – and it may well, by then, have become an annual custom – members of the gild of St Mary went in procession to St Mary's church with lighted candles, headed by people costumed to represent Mary, Joseph, Simeon and two angels. Mary bore an effigy of Jesus and presented the child to Simeon at the high altar.

It has been claimed that the Beverley plays continued to be produced until the early years of the 17th century but, although there may well have been some attempt to resuscitate them during the reign of Mary (1553-58), there would appear to be no reference to them after 1541. Like much else, they died with the changes of the Reformation.

According to John Leland, who must have visited Beverley c.1540, the town as a whole was 'large and well builded of wood'. But little of this early timber-framed building survives apart from what today may be seen in a garage* on the west side of North Bar Within and at the Sun Inn in Flemingate. No doubt, as elsewhere, there have been refacings of early structures which have undergone a Georgian or later face-lift. Much of the so-called 'heritage area'† of the town, however, dates from the 17th century and later.

Contrary to what has often been asserted, Beverley has always been an 'open' town and was never walled as were York and Hull. It is true that, because of Scottish incursions into northern England after the English

---

* Converted into St Mary's Court, a shopping arcade, in 1983.
† Designated as a conservation area in 1968.

15th-century timber-framed building in North Bar Within, now St Mary's Court.

*North Bar
1409-10,
photographed
c.1938.*

*Newbegin Bar,
demolished
1790.*

*Keldgate Bar,
demolished
1808.*

disaster at Bannockburn (1314), Beverley – like Hull – was accorded royal licence in 1321 to fortify. But, if a system of defence towers linked by curtain walling was ever seriously envisaged, there is no evidence that an attempt was made to implement such plans. Unlike Hull, the town received no grants of murage, that is, officially accorded rights to impose special tolls on goods for defensive works. This would certainly have been the case if an enormously expensive defence programme had been embarked upon. Yet in the middle years of the 15th century, four bars – North, Newbegin, Keldgate (South), and Norwood Bars controlled the main roads into the town: only the first three of these survived into the 16th century. Despite the quasi-military character as evidenced in the surviving North Bar, these bars, without linking curtain walling, could have performed no useful function beyond control of entrance and exit, facility for the collection of toll, and the restriction of movement in time of plague, pestilence and local upset. Yet it is worth remarking that both North and Newbegin Bars were built in 1409-10. Henry IV was in Beverley in 1408 and again in 1410 and one might be tempted to see in this rebuilding the beginnings of a belated attempt, with royal approval, to strengthen the site of the town following the unsuccessful rebellion of the Percies which ended with the defeat and death of Henry, the fourth Lord Percy, at the Battle of Bramham Moor early in 1408.

The Newbegin and Keldgate Bars were demolished in comparatively modern times, the former in 1790 and the latter, which was apparently in a state of chronic disrepair, in 1808. The North Bar, the curve of the archway of which until recently determined the unusual coved roofing of many East Yorkshire Motor Services double-decker buses, has suffered progressive laceration and scarring from traffic, and substantial repair has been necessary after unduly belated official appraisal of a problem of preservation which was clearly evident in the 1950s. The Bar is the earliest surviving brick gateway of its type in the country and, as extant accounts testify, it was built of Beverley-made bricks at a total cost to the town of £96. 17s. 4½d. It replaced an earlier structure, and collections were made in the town to supplement the Corporation expenditure necessary. Walter Dunham, the Town Clerk, gave a shilling towards lead for the Bar (presumably for the roof) and William Scarborough, the vicar of St Mary's, donated 20 shillings and also bought the timber door of what was, probably, the earlier gateway for a similar sum. Some 20 local brickmakers, including Agnes (the) Tiler and the inelegantly named John Mudfysch, supplied the 112,300 bricks required: the cost of these at contemporary prices, worked out at about 3s. 8d. per 1,000. And while this work on the North Bar was going ahead, the west towers of Beverley Minster were gradually rising and the west towers of York Minster had yet to be begun.

The observation of the scholar, F. W. Maitland, that 'those who would study the early history of our towns . . . have fields and pastures on their hands' is appropriately applicable to Beverley. The history of Beverley's common lands, which *in toto* amount to nearly 1,200 acres, cannot be surveyed in detail here but it is important that their economic and social significance to the medieval town community should not go unnoticed.

East and south-east of the town and aligning the River Hull are the pastures of Swinemoor and Figham (with Lund): before 1500 the town also possessed, at the end of the Beck, another pasture known as the Tonge. Until the disciplining of the River Hull in the 18th century and the making of the Beverley and Barmston Low Level Drain after 1798, large areas of these eastern pastures must have been flooded waste for much of the year. Economic exploitation would have been largely confined to fishing and fowling, although by raising of banks some degree of protection was given from inundation, thereby providing some pasture above flood level. As the Lord of Beverley, Archbishop Sewell de Boville c.1258 had given the men of Beverley rights of common in Figham but it is not known how rights of common in Swinemoor were secured to the medieval burgesses. By the 14th century, however, the Archbishop's villeins of nearby Stork and Sandholme within St John's Liberties had recognised rights in the pasture and it is a reasonable inference that by then the town's burgesses also had rights there.

Westwood and Hurn, to the west of the town, effectively one main pasture, were far more important and valuable than Swinemoor and Figham. This wold land presented no problems of drainage and embankment and its exploitation by digging for chalk and clay has helped to enhance the natural beauty of this once heavily-wooded heath by providing an even more variegated scene. The origin of burgess rights in the 'Westwood' is historically more easily discernible than in the case of Figham and Swinemoor.

There had been considerable bitterness c.1200 between the men of Beverley and Archbishop Geoffrey Plantagenet over pasture rights. About 1258 Archbishop Sewell de Boville effected an agreement with the burgesses whereby they surrendered their rights in the Archbishop's park, south of the Minster (Beverley Parks), which the Archbishop wished to empark for hunting purposes. In return the Archbishop granted the borough community certain rights of common in the West Wood of Beverley as well as in Figham. On the face of it, this would have seemed to be a reasonably fair exchange but it is clear that the burgesses resented the loss of their ancient rights in Beverley Parks and numerous inquiries were necessary into subsequent archiepiscopal complaints of loss and damage there as the result of burgess trespass and poaching.

A second agreement in almost identical terms was made in 1282 with Archbishop William Wickwane, but with the additional bait for the burgesses, for an annual rent of 6s. 8d., of a property in the Market Place called 'Byscopdynges': this was the hall of the archbishops in Beverley which was thus apparently made available for communal use. But, despite this, complaints of burgess trespass continued and a reasonable degree of stability in relationships between the townspeople and their archbishop overlord over rights of pasture was not achieved until 1379-80. Reserving certain rights for himself and his tenants of Bishop Burton, Archbishop Alexander Neville granted in perpetuity to the twelve Keepers and the commonalty, subject to an annual rental payment of 100 shillings, what was described as 'un boys appelle Westwod de Beverlee' [i.e. a wood called Beverley Westwood]. This rent continued to be paid to the archbishops until Archbishop Edward Lee in 1543, under duress, surrendered to the Crown his lands and ancient manorial rights in Beverley in return for lands which had formerly belonged to certain recently dissolved monasteries in the North Riding.

Another pasture right enjoyed by the burgesses was that of 'averidge' , that is the right to the 'fog'* after hay had been lifted. These rights extended over certain early enclosures and crofts which were in due course leased out by the Corporation. 'Averidge' on these was not finally extinguished, by the device of composition payments, until the late 17th century: the last recorded sale of rights of 'averidge' was that on the Keldgate Leases to Abigail Johnson in 1684 for £10.

Until the Pastures Act of 1836 the administration of the pastures was wholly in the hands of the Corporation, who selected the pasture masters from their own body. Within his 'stint' every burgess had rights of pasture for his animals and it was the responsibility of the pasture masters to arrange accordingly. Later records testify concern at the incidence of fraud and imposition over the exceeding of individual stints and of burgesses passing off others' animals as their own.

Westwood chalk was used both as a foundation for Beverley's streets and for the making of lime. Limekilns on the Westwood were in operation until 1812 and their leasing out by the Corporation provided a useful and regular source of income for the town. Clay, too, was excavated for brickmaking, and the pits, hillocks and hollows in the pasture today, especially in those parts nearest the town, testify to this exploitation of mineral wealth. And, of course, both Westwood and Hurn were progressively denuded of trees and bushes, as the extensive woodland naturally provided building timber and fuel. When borough finances were straitened, trees could always be felled and sold off: Hurn, for example, was finally cleared of trees shortly before 1700 because at the time the civic purse was sadly depleted.

With occasional variation, the rule of the town was in the hands of a council of twelve Keepers, with safeguards against possible oligarchic development by a rule that a Keeper was ineligible for immediate re-election on expiry of his term of office. Some element of continuity was assured by the outgoing Keepers nominating 18 other *probiores* [approved candidates] for the election of 12 by the burgesses-at-large. The system had its ups and downs and, as at York and Scarborough, for example, there was

---

* The long grass left standing.

considerable upset and rioting in 1381,* but a tradition of consultation by Keepers with the *communitas* [commonalty] continued. Civic rule in Beverley contrasts markedly with the narrow oligarchical rule of 13 Aldermen in Hull, a system which was stabilised by charter in 1440 and continued until municipal corporation reform in 1835. Unlike many boroughs, Beverley had no mayor as such until 1573, but the responsibility of civic leadership appears to have devolved on the Keeper who headed the poll at the annual election: during the ensuing year he was clearly *primus inter pares* [first among equals].

Despite a town economy based on trade and industry, it is clear from the foregoing that the agricultural element was more than apparent. Sheep had ancient rights to herbage in the streets: records here as elsewhere show that the pig was a ubiquitous animal but, if impounded roaming the streets, was likely to cost its owner a fine of twopence – a regulation, incidentally, which did not apply to swine with litter or en route to pasture in the charge of the town's swineherd. Butchers' dogs were apparently unusually vicious beasts and in 1367 it was ordered that, if one was caught at large, or bit a stranger's pig or dog, its owner would be penalised to the extent of 3s. 4d., which was exactly half the fine he would have paid for abusing the Town Clerk.

Life for the townsman at times could be nasty and brutish, and riot and disturbance was by no means infrequent. For example, market arrangements were such that it was found advisable to position the fishmongers between the town's butchers and 'stranger' butchers, lest, in the delicious phrasing of the town's ordinance of 1409, 'the butchers should intermeddle with each other'. The known fact, too, that the Minster had ancient chartered rights of sanctuary inevitably attracted a criminal element into the town and, although this did not necessarily make the town an urban Botany Bay, it must have contributed in some measure to violence and instability.

We have no knowledge of how badly the town was hit by the great plague of 1349 or by subsequent outbreaks within the medieval period. Four-fifths of the monastic community at nearby Meaux were wiped out in 1349 and, although virulence varied from area to area, it is not beyond the bounds of possibility that in Beverley, some 2,000 people perished in the pestilence. Despite the paucity of illustrative evidence it would be justifiable to assume that civic orders in matters of public health and much else were often little more than pious statements of intention which, too often, went unfulfilled. There is no doubt that irresponsible townspeople who, in defiance of town ordinance, washed hides in the ditch near Wolfkeld, threw rubbish in the Walker Beck or dumped their muck in the streets so that it was both a nuisance to the public and a danger to nearby walls, still continued to offend when opportunity served.

---

* The year of the Peasants' Revolt.

The overall picture of medieval Beverley, therefore, is of a town and borough developing on a manor of the archbishops of York, dominated, but not wholly overawed, by the rich as represented by the archbishop and the provost and canons of the Minster. It is one, too, of a town which reached its maximum growth as a trading and clothmaking centre before 1400 and thereafter began a progressive decline as competition from the West Riding clothing towns of Wakefield, Halifax, Bradford and Leeds began to build up. By the early 16th century, to quote John Leland, the one-time 'good cloth making at Beverley' was 'much decayed'. To that may be added the fact that the years of the Reformation brought radical change in other ways to the town: how Beverley fared in the age of the Tudors and early Stuarts will be considered in due course.

Beverley Minster.

3. BEVERLEY AND THE MEDIEVAL CHURCH

Although there are no details extant of the pre-Conquest organisation of the Minster, it is possible that the 'corporation' or 'chapter' of clergy or secular canons established by Athelstan to serve the Minster church was seven in number. There were seven canons at Lichfield and apparently seven at York originally. The number is traditionally explained by reference to the seven deacons, the 'seven men of good reputation . . . full of the spirit and wisdom' who (*vide* Acts VI, v.1-6) were appointed to 'wait at table' or, in other words, to administer the temporal concerns of the early church. With the development of a capitular organisation at Beverley, each canon was provided with a 'benefice' – a prebend which was named after one of the altars in the church. The prebend represented the fruits of a specific portion of the Minster's propertied endowments which, on the evidence of the Domesday Survey of 1086, were considerable. Thus a canon was officially 'Canon of the church of St John at Beverley and prebendary of the prebend of (e.g. St Martin) in the same'. These seven prebends at Beverley (those of St Martin, the Blessed Virgin Mary, St Peter, St Andrew, St Stephen, St James and St Michael) were not equal in value: by far the most valuable was that of St Martin and, as such, was much sought after. At some unknown date or dates in the 13th century two further prebends were added – those of St Katherine and St Leonard, the latter being held successively by the archbishops of York: these new prebends clearly reflected greater endowments and rising revenues. The canons had obligations of residence but many prebendaries were virtually permanent absentees, the prebends being held in plurality with other benefices and often by king's clerks who were away on royal business for long periods and had the necessary dispensation from residence. In fact c.1300 only three canons-prebendary were resident and they come to notice in record at that time because of allegations about their personal conduct.

Each canon had a vicar known as a vicar choral whose duties were to officiate on his behalf in his absence and take a full part in the maintenance of the daily round of services. Additionally at Beverley there were seven Clerks of the Barfel (*Berefellarii*), probably so-called because of their bearskin-tipped gowns. These were young men enjoying what was tantamount to ecclesiastical 'exhibitions': they were bound to continual residence although they could, and often did, get leave to study at the universities. Because the name *berefellarii* invited ridicule (bearskins/bareskins), Archbishop Thomas Arundel, in his Statutes of 1391 for the Minster, decreed that henceforth they were to be referred to as parsons. The medieval Minster clergy also included chantry priests serving the various altars at which chantries had been established and some 17 'Clerks of the Second Form'. As in other medieval collegiate churches there was, by modern standards, a formidable array of clergy in their various grades and categories. At the time of the dissolution of the collegiate church of St John in 1548 under the Chantries Statute of the previous year, the 'staff establishment', including 8 choristers, was 77.

Had Beverley Minster been a cathedral church, there would have been four dignitaries – dean, chancellor, precentor and treasurer – taking precedence of their fellow canons in chapter. But at Beverley the constitution, reflecting probably early organisation, was somewhat different. There were precentor, sacrist (treasurer) and chancellor, all bound to continual residence, but these officers were distinct from the canons and ranked below them. The chancellor, usually a vicar-choral, was the legal officer to the Chapter and was ex-officio head of the Minster Grammar School which, no doubt in medieval times, as later, occupied a position in the south-west corner of the Minster churchyard. The precentor, as his name implies, was in charge of the choir and song school, and the sacrist had responsibility for the services, books and valuables. But, constitutionally, the most interesting officer of all was the provost, who appointed the precentor, chancellor and sacrist and paid them out of the revenue of the provostry. The provost himself did not hold a canonry just because he was provost nor, by virtue of his office, had he a stall in choir or voice in chapter. Although exceptions do occur, he was usually a canon and therefore held a prebend in his own right. His office – familiar on the Continent – was probably brought into being by the necessity of the chapter having to have a procurator to manage the revenues and estates. His appointment at Beverley followed the example of York where, on the evidence of Hugh the Chantor, Archbishop Thomas de Bayeux (1070-1100) appointed such an officer: but at York, unlike Beverley, the office of provost did not persist. The first recorded provost of Beverley was Thomas the Younger, nephew of Archbishop Thomas de Bayeux, who was appointed in the last years of his uncle's archiepiscopate.

The 'benefice' of provost at Beverley was a lucrative one and therefore much sought after. In fact many well-known medieval ecclesiastics – Roger de Pont l'Evêque (Archbishop of York 1154-81), Thomas Becket, Fulk Bassett (Bishop of London 1244-59), William de Melton (Archbishop of York 1316-40) and Thomas Winter, the illegitimate son of Cardinal Wolsey, among them – were provosts of Beverley in their day. Winter's case is an interesting example of how the provostry could be used. When Wolsey was at the height of his power, in addition to being provost of Beverley, Thomas Winter was also a canon of Lincoln, York, Southwell and Beverley, archdeacon of Norfolk, archdeacon of Suffolk, archdeacon of Salisbury, dean of Wells, rector of Rudby (North Riding) and rector of St Matthew's, Ipswich. While enjoying these benefices the young man was being educated by tutors in Paris, spending his money freely and not getting on too well with his Latin.

An early sacrist of the Minster was the historian Alured who c.1145, during the troublous times of Stephen and Matilda, compiled the *Annals or History of the Kings of England down to the year 1129*. Although not without interest in its own right, there is little in Alured's *History* that is original, for in typical medieval fashion he incorporated into his text substantial extracts from the works of other historians and chroniclers like Bede, Symeon of Durham and Henry of Huntingdon: his work throws no light on early Minster history. Traditionally he is said to have collected and translated all the Minster's charters from the English (i.e. Anglo-Saxon) into Latin: one might therefore be tempted to speculate if, in his day, he was personally acquainted with the original charter of Athelstan.

The medieval chapter's relationships with the archbishops of York were not always harmonious. When troubles arose it was usually over matters of relative rights and jurisdictions. In the time of Archbishop Alexander Neville of York (1374-88), 'the fiery prelate', the greater part of the canons and vicars choral literally went on strike and the archbishop was compelled to import blackleg ecclesiastical labour from York to keep the services going. But Beverley Minster Chapter was by no means the only ecclesiastical corporation with which Neville quarrelled.

★ ★ ★

As will have been deduced from the details given in Chapter 1, the Beverley Minster of 1066 was, one would think, a largish and relatively new church with a recently built presbytery, an imposing tower and a nave of unknown date but probably not more than half a century old. As will be seen in due course, there is reason to think that in 1066 or by the end of the 11th century the church could have been cruciform in plan.

There is nothing in any extant medieval chronicle or record about any rebuilding programme at Beverley in the 12th century, yet, considering the immensity of the building contribution of the Normans within a century and a half of the Conquest, it is scarcely credible that in that period there could have been no 'Normanising' of the Minster fabric. The fabric does, however, bear indications of Norman work: the apparent re-use of 12th-century ashlar in the eastern half of the present church, re-used chevroned stone in the 14th-century nave triforium, and the existence of a Norman font are all pointers to the possibility of building work of importance being carried out in the 12th century. Although, of course, absolute proof is lacking, it is possible that the Norman building contribution at Beverley was a replacement of the pre-Conquest nave and the addition of transepts. But in fairly quick succession there came two serious disasters. As both Roger de Hoveden (Howden) and the author of *Gesta Regis Henrici Secundi* tell us, 'the whole town of Beverley together with the noble church of the Blessed John the Archbishop was burnt' on the eve of St Matthew, 20 September 1188. According to a Latin inscription on a lead plate in the vault in the floor of the nave where John's reputed relics lie (and which, incidentally, puts the disaster as being on the night after the feast of St Matthew, 1188), a search was made for John's remains but they were not found until 1197. This suggests a major disaster affecting the eastern part of the church where John's shrine would be placed, for a search for the shrine and its holy relics would have had a high priority in any clearing-up process.

The second calamity came c.1213. An anonymous historian of York, relating a miracle of St John, records that the canons were minded to place on the tower built by Cynesige 'a roof of stonework of proportionate beauty' but the craftsmen engaged on the work were not as cautious as they should have been. Setting up the four piers to carry the whole mass was like 'sewing new cloth into old'. Cracks in bases and shafts appeared and ruin threatened so that many would not go into church. One October morning a priest, apparently suffering from insomnia, rang the bell for matins an hour too soon. When the canons assembled in choir some stones fell from the tower: after a second fall of stone they wisely moved to the west end of the nave and finished the service there. They had scarcely returned to their houses when the great tower collapsed. For the unknown chronicler who relates all this, the point was that, once again, it was thanks to the intercession of St John of Beverley that disaster to life and limb had been averted.

For us today, the importance of the story lies in the possible architectural deductions which may be made about the church. The stone roof work referred to would appear to have been a vault which, if 'of proportionate beauty and height' on a 'very high tower of astonishing beauty and size' must itself have been a work of some magnitude. Secondly, the tower is described as being 'in the midst of the crossing', which suggests that the earlier Minster was transeptal. Thirdly, the fact that the canons completed their service at the west end of the nave clearly suggests that it was the choir which was threatened by a possible fall of the tower. That the choir was badly damaged or destroyed by the fall of the central tower may also be deduced from the fact that when rebuilding began it was from the east end. All this is interestingly borne out by a possible slightly later reference which might be dated to c.1217-20. A crucifixion play was being performed on the north side of the church – incidentally the earliest known reference to a liturgical play in a churchyard in England. Some boys climbed up inside the church to see the play more easily and were chased out by the sexton. One fell but, thanks to the intercession of St John, miraculously descended safely to earth and escaped without injury. This escapade, which seems to embody a substratum of truth, is more likely to have been a boyish incursion within the nave rather than the choir. If this deduction be correct and if the alleged incident post-dated the fall of the tower, then the (Norman?) nave was still standing, although in a fall of the tower eastwards it is difficult to believe that the nave itself could have been wholly undamaged.

The rebuilding which was necessary after these two disasters has given us the present noble fabric. In usual fashion, royal Letters Patent of Protection were periodically accorded the Minster clergy, the first being dated 6 November, 1221. Archbishop Walter de Grey of York in 1232 granted relaxation of 20 days' enjoined penance to all those who, being contrite, contributed to the rebuilding of the church, then *'miserabili ruina (et) enormiter deformata'* [a wretched ruin and extremely dilapidated]. In 1252 a royal precept to Geoffrey de Langley, Justiciar of Forests, for the delivery of 40 oaks from Sherwood Forest for the works at Beverley Minster could suggest that, by that date, new works were up to roof level. Probably by c.1270 this first great building campaign, which comprised choir, greater and lesser transepts, chapter house (now destroyed) and the beginnings of the east end of the nave, was completed.

We have no knowledge of the identity of the master mason or masons who, by his great work, set the scale for the fabric as a whole, but if a guess were to be made – and it can be nothing more – then the name of Robert de Beverley, king's master mason from 1261, who was engaged on work at Westminster Abbey, the Tower of London, Windsor Castle and elsewhere, cannot be wholly discounted. Another who could have been associated with building at Beverley was Alexander the Mason, who was working at Worcester c.1236-40 and at Lincoln c.1240, for in a number of architectural respects Beverley is very much a daughter church of Lincoln. But these are only suggestions of possibilities: the record evidence to provide both the answer and the proof is lacking.

The next major building campaign, which began in 1308 and involved the replacement of the nave, was preceded by the making of a yet more magnificent shrine to contain the relics of St John. In 1292 the chapter contracted with Roger of Faringdon, a London goldsmith, to make a shrine five and a half feet long, one and a half feet wide 'and of proportionate height': the chapter was to provide the silver and gold which Roger was to refine as necessary. It was to be: 'beautiful and fit with plates and columns of masons' work and figures of cunning and beautiful work . . . appropriate for a shrine of this sort and beauty such as belong to goldsmiths' work'.

The chapter reserved the right to reject any figure or ornament which appeared unsuitable, in which case Roger was to remake it without any additional charge: in any case, as part of the contract, he was to do no other work until the shrine was complete. We do not know when it was finished, but in 1305 a certain John the Goldsmith was also concerned with it. It is likely to have been finished by 1308 for by then there are no further references to collections for the shrine and in the summer of that year Archbishop William Greenfield dedicated the high altar in honour of St John of Beverley. This sumptuous shrine, which no doubt occupied a place of honour immediately behind the high altar, was carried in procession throughout the town at Rogationtide.

Meanwhile, money was coming in for the building of the nave, and the canons were issuing certificates testifying to the restoration to health of those who, being sick, had visited the shrine. It was said that Agnes of Sherburn-in-Elmet, brought to Beverley raving mad, had recovered at the shrine in 1318. Four years later, John, the dumb son of William of Ferriby, had his voice restored; he then went blind so was rushed back to Beverley, recovered his sight at the tomb and apparently provided appropriate conclusive evidence that a miracle had occurred by reading the psalm, '0, praise the Lord with me'. The next year, Maud of Settrington, so crippled that she could only go about on her hands, spent three weeks at the tomb and was said to have been fully restored to health. Clearly there was a very real propaganda and financial value in these well-publicised stories.

It is possible that the Minster master mason, Oliver de Stainefield, was initially concerned with the nave building programme for in 1305, having been given leave of absence by the chapter at the request of Henry de Lacy, Earl of Lincoln, he was then being urgently recalled to duty: as Henry de Lacy is known as the builder of Denbigh Castle, it is possible that Oliver was working there at the time. There are also notices of other master masons between 1322 and 1335 – Ralph of Whitby, William de la Mare and William de Malton of Huggate – all these, too, in almost anonymous fashion and to a greater or lesser degree, must have been involved with the building of the nave. It could be that the work on the new nave with its brick filled vault was substantially completed by the time of the Black Death (1349) but there is no proof and it would be unwise to speculate too precisely on the year when the whole work was finished. It may be that completion, in any real sense, was delayed until well into the 1360s.

The third and last major building programme seems to have begun c.1390: the gift of 20 oaks from South Burton (Bishop Burton) Wood by Archbishop Alexander Neville a little before 1388 suggests that a further building programme was contemplated despite the ecclesiastical upsets at the time. The evidence of one or two contemporary wills also lends support to the possibility that a building project was getting under way. It is generally accepted that this last phase, which gave us the elegant west towers and west front, the north porch of the nave and certain other work towards the west end, lasted over a generation and was probably completed by c.1420. In these years, too, there were modifications elsewhere to the fabric: the great east window, for example, can be dated fairly closely to c.1416 for it was in that year that William de Waltham, canon both of Beverley and York, bequeathed £40 towards its construction. The last addition modifying the ground plan of the church came in 1489-90 with the building of a chapel at the east end of the north aisle of the choir to contain the remains of Henry Percy, 4th Earl of Northumberland, who was murdered by a riotous mob at Cocklodge, near Thirsk, on 28 April 1489. His particularly sumptuous funeral and the building of a special chapel to accommodate his remains were appropriate to the head of the great northern House of Percy. By c.1500, then, apart from the facts that there was a chapter house on the north side, a chapel of St Martin at the south-west corner and an octagonal lantern on the central stub tower, the Minster church, externally, looked very much as it does today. The small octagon lasted until the early years of the 18th century when, as a result of the reconstruction of the upper part of the tower at the crossing, it was inconsiderately replaced by a classical cupola: this external excrescence was removed in 1824.

Despite the fact that the Minster fabric as we see it today is the result of three medieval building campaigns of the 13th, 14th and 15th centuries, the whole church has a remarkable architectural unity. The 14th-century builders were conservatively minded and continued the 13th-century triforium design, the blind wall arcade of the nave aisles and the original steep 13th-century roof pitch. As a result, although the architectural detail alters, the general impression through such a marriage of styles is one of unity. Furthermore, there are many aesthetically pleasing features about the church, such as that of the solution of the problem of approach to the former medieval octagonal chapter house from the north aisle of the choir. This was done by resolving the blank wall arcade into a dual stairwayed approach: the conception of such a design was an inspiration in itself.

Of the major furnishings of this great church, the Percy Tomb canopy is one of the treasures of western medieval Gothic art. It is more likely to be the canopied tomb of Lady Idonea Percy (d.1365), daughter of Robert, the first Lord Clifford, and wife of Henry, the second Lord Percy of Alnwick, than that of her mother-in-law, Lady Eleanor, wife of Henry, the first Lord Percy. The table tomb was clearly designed to support an Easter Sepulchre. Linked with the tomb canopy is the 14th-century reredos and platform, sympathetically restored by William Comins, the master mason of the Minster, 1813-37. This was considerably embellished with mosaic work and figures by Canon H. E. Nolloth at the end of the 19th century in memory of his father, Henry Ovenden Nolloth. A tomb of approximately similar date is placed between the south aisle piers in the western half of the nave. Below, on modern supports, is a substantial slab of marble which, by reason of its measurements, may well have been the base which supported the medieval shrine of St John: clearly, it is not *in situ*. In the sanctuary north of the altar, and doubtless dating from the earliest years of the Minster's history, is the famous *frithstol* or sanctuary chair. Lacking any positive dating criteria it nevertheless provides assurance that it is one of the most venerable of English church furnishings and, in point of age, is the Minster's most precious relic.

The fine set of canopied stalls in the choir, the work of the so-called Ripon School of wood carvers, was completed only a generation before the dissolution of the collegiate church: the woodwork is excellent testimony to Yorkshire artistic skill and craftsmanship. These Beverley stalls have a close affinity with those in the cathedrals of Manchester and Ripon. The 68 misericords, or corbelled-out subsidiary seats beneath the tip-up seats of each stall, provide a wealth of illustrative material of secular life as well as showing a cartoonist propensity for cynical and humorous comment on the contemporary scene. Many of the misericord themes are incidents of everyday life such as that of the domestic cameo of the unfortunate husband being unmercifully belaboured by his termagant wife while a dog, in canine opportunist fashion, sneaks in and, as discord continues, puts its head in the momentarily forgotten cooking pot on the floor. This particular incident has its sequel in the misericord of the next stall for there the militant shrew is presumably being led to the ducking stool to be cooled off. Other misericords, like the fox attired in friar's garb, are more recondite in type.

It is easy to eulogise a building such as Beverley Minster simply because in so many ways and like many another great church of its period, it is a remarkably impressive essay both within and without in building technique, craftsmanship and artistic expression. The sullen, heavy and sheer masculinity of Norman Romanesque as seen at Durham, Tewkesbury, Winchester or Ely, and which no doubt characterised much of the earlier Minster church at Beverley, has here been replaced by a superlative example of Gothic elegance and grace which dominates town and countryside for miles around: there can be few now who would regret the 13th-century decision to rebuild.

*   *   *

One of the interesting points about the medieval history of the Minster is that each prebendal altar carried with it 'parish' responsibilities: but the 'cure of souls' annexed to the altars had no parochial boundaries as such except probably in the case of the prebend of St Martin, on the lands of which there was built a chapel of St Mary. The properties of that prebend included a greater part of Beverley to the north. Inevitably, therefore, with the development of the town, the chapel of St Mary, dependent on the altar of St Martin in the Minster, would assume a greater importance with increased emphasis placed on it by the merchant class and townspeople in general. This fact was recognised in 1269 when Archbishop Walter Giffard, on the grounds that it was 'not expedient to muzzle the ox which treadeth the corn', instituted a vicarage* by deed of ordination allocating emoluments thereto of £23. 6s. 8d. a year – approximately one quarter of the total value of the prebend of St Martin. Roger de Rise was instituted as first vicar. Complete independence of the Minster, of course, did not follow. While the vicar and his successors were bound to serve the cure, they were to be present at certain Minster processions and to swear obedience to the Canon of St Martin who, at the time of the institution of Roger de Rise, was Gilbert of St Leofard, afterwards Bishop of Chichester (1288). But, despite the legal position, it is understandable that with the inevitable development of St Mary as the town's 'parish church', feelings of dependence on the Minster would naturally lessen, and certainly by the early years of the 14th century some evidence of independence of spirit is

---

* Not a building, but a benefice held by a priest.

St Mary's church, 1853.

manifest by the warnings issued by the Minster Chapter to the Vicar of St Mary's and the priests there to attend the Minster processions.

It is not known when the first chapel of St Mary's was built. In the 16th century John Leland, king's antiquary and librarian, recorded the tradition that St Mary's owed its beginnings to Archbishop Thurstan of York who, with the consent of the Minster Chapter of canons, established a chapel of St Mary and also a chapel of St Thomas, the latter being outside the Keldgate Bar. There are references to the chapel of St Thomas as late as the 15th century but there is no record of when it ceased to exist as a chapel. The establishment of these two chapels by Thurstan may well have been the case but in the absence of record a later pious ascription to Thurstan, who has some justification for being regarded as one of the town's founding fathers, is understandable.

There can be few churches in England which have endured so much change, addition, restoration and rebuilding as St Mary's, Beverley. Early work, re-used, lies cheek by jowl with later, testifying in many instances to the substantial rebuild which followed the 'fall' of the church in 1520 when a number of people were killed. Earliest surviving material – Norman chevroned stone and squared ashlar – does, unless it has been brought from elsewhere, clearly attest to the 12th-century building origins of the present fabric. Few ecclesiologists would care to deny that the church of Beverley St Mary is one of the finest parish churches in England and one which poses fascinating and intriguing architectural problems. Therein lies much of its charm. From the 13th century onwards it became very much the church of the medieval clothing gilds, the mercers, drapers and weavers, as well as of others, and the many bequests of medieval Beverley merchants clearly attest the affection in which it was held.

The chapel of St Thomas was founded on the prebendal lands of St Michael. When Thomas Becket was provost of Beverley (c.1154), he also held the prebend of St Michael and presumably continued to enjoy his benefice until he became archbishop of Canterbury in 1162. Becket was murdered on the altar steps of his cathedral in 1170. He was canonised in 1172 and in 1220 his remains were translated to a shrine in Trinity Chapel in Canterbury Cathedral, a shrine which, as readers of Chaucer well know, became a great centre of medieval pilgrimage. According to Simon Russell who, c.1415, compiled the Provosts Book of the Minster, the chapel of St Thomas outside Keldgate Bar became more frequented after St Thomas Becket's translation in 1220 because of its historical association with the saint. There is the implication here of popular confusion between St Thomas the Apostle and St Thomas the Martyr. Although the reference in the Provosts Book is specifically to the chapel of St Thomas the Apostle, the historian might dare to suggest that, writing two and a half centuries later, Simon Russell may have been mistaken and that the chapel founded on the lands of the prebend of St Michael was in fact in honour of the martyred archbishop and not of the Apostle. If such a theory be correct, then the foundation of the chapel at the instance of Archbishop Thurstan must be ruled out.

Beverley's 'port' at the Beck also had its church, which may well have achieved a degree of independence of the collegiate church of St John earlier than St Mary's. The earliest reference the existence of a church of St Nicholas – omitting the well-worn and wholly unauthenticated local tradition that it was built by John of Beverley – is c.1160 when a certain Thorold, priest of St Nicholas, appears as a witness to a charter to the convent of Swine in Holderness. The site of this medieval church, often referred to as the Holme Church of St Nicholas, was excavated just before the Second World War.* The old church stood approximately 80 yards south-east of the modern church: the site has now been built over. Excavation clearly showed that the area had been sadly plundered of building stone and this accords with what is known historically. The little medieval church declined with the decay of Beverley's cloth trade and by the time of the outbreak of the Civil War in 1642 the end had come, although the tower was apparently left standing for some years. Stone was almost certainly used for fortifications, and on the evidence of the borough records much seems to have been used,

---

* This excavation was undertaken in 1938 by Robert H. Carr and Kenneth A. MacMahon (see 'The Excavation of the Holme Church of St Nicholas, Beverley' *Yorkshire Archaeological Journal*), Part 136, vol.xxxiv, (1939), pp.399-410.

too, for the repair of both the Minster and St Mary's in the 17th century. And there can be little doubt that stone used for the repair of the banks of the nearby Beck also came from the same site.

*   *   *

There were two houses of friars in medieval Beverley. The Dominicans, or Black Friars, were established here within a generation of the founding of the Order by Dominic Guzman, inasmuch as a provincial chapter of the order is known to have been held at Beverley in 1240. That a friary building programme was in hand c.1260 is suggested by the fact that in 1263 Henry III gave the community a substantial gift of 15 oaks from the Forest of Galtres, north of York. By the early years of the 14th century the community numbered as many as 42 brethren, and the long 14th- and 15th-century record of gifts and bequests from members of the important Yorkshire families of Vavasour, Percy, Constable, Wake and Darcy, as well as from humble Beverley burgesses, testifies to the high regard in which the friars were held.

The friary and nearby hospital of St Nicholas lay immediately to the north-east of the Minster and on the north side of the narrow street known as Friars Lane which, by way of Hellegarth Lane (now stopped up), led

The Dominican Friary, photographed 1973. Now a Youth Hostel.

down to Beckside. The cloister was on the north of the spacious friary church, the greater part of the foundations of which presumably still lie, relatively undisturbed, below the railway to the east. The surviving fragment, which would probably represent the dormitory and library which were built following a disastrous fire in 1449, was put to secular use after the dissolution of the house in 1539 and was added to c.1580. From the early 19th century until after 1960 the building was divided into three dwellings, and, with its red-brick boundary wall and charming 15th-century gateways, worthily enhanced the Minster precincts. Today, as these words are penned, the building stands pathetic, forlorn and desolate – grim evidence of 20th-century official vandalism and planned neglect.*

North-west of the Keldgate Bar and west of the town ditch (the line of which is marked by the modern road known as The Leases) was the Franciscan friary. It is not known precisely when the Franciscans first arrived in Beverley but a friary was in existence in 1267 on a site probably within the town itself. In 1297 lands contiguous to a chapel of St Elena seem to have been gifted to the Beverley Franciscans by William Lyketon and Henry Wygthon resulting in a virtual re-foundation of the house on a site near the Keldgate Bar. Although in the early 14th century the community was about the same viable size as that of the Dominican friary, communal misfortune seems to have dogged it and within two or three years of the Black Death (1349) there was a second re-foundation at the instance of Sir John Hotham of Scorborough. The Hothams continued to be benefactors and several members of the family were buried in the friary church. When the friary was surrendered to the Crown early in 1539 it is recorded as occupying some seven acres of land on this site west of the town. The area is now completely built over.

Thanks to the gift in 1201 by Sybil de Valloines, widow of Ralph d'Aubigny, of the manor of Holy Trinity and other properties, the Knights Hospitaller were able to establish a preceptory at Beverley in the early years of the 13th century. The moated site of the Hospitallers, later more popularly known as the Trinities (giving its name to nearby Trinity Lane), was largely obliterated by the building of the railway and railway station in 1846. Not a great deal is known of the history of the preceptory which on the eve of its dissolution in 1540 was among the wealthiest houses of the order. In 1576 the site was bought by the town Corporation and the surviving building usefully served as a pest house for the isolation of plague victims as occasion required. As a result, as building has proceeded in more recent times, and especially in the area between Cherry Tree Lane and the railway, there has been inevitable disturbance of burials, many of them no doubt of 17th-century plague victims.†

---

* Restored by the Beverley Friary Preservation Trust, the building was opened as a Youth Hostel in 1984.
† An archaeological investigation was undertaken in 1989.

At least some of the town's sick, aged and impotent poor were cared for by various religious foundations broadly referred to as hospitals, a term not to be precisely equated with its modern meaning: the function of the medieval hospital was care rather than cure. Beverley's oldest hospital was that of St Giles, which was sited outside the Newbegin Bar, south-west of present-day Westwood Road, and therefore somewhat to the north of the Grey Friars.*

According to John Leland it was founded 'by one Wuse' before the Norman Conquest but a 16th-century record of early tradition can hardly be construed as a registration of hard historical fact. By the second half of the 13th century the hospital had fallen on evil times and, in 1277, in the interests of good rule and governance, Archbishop Walter Giffard annexed it with all its properties to the Augustinian priory of Warter, near Pocklington. At about this time the hospital was organised for 4 priest-brethren, 6 sick priests and 15 sick people, both men and women. Later it was not unknown for a woman to be admitted as a recluse.

Thus from 1277 the history of the Beverley hospital of St Giles merges with that of Warter Priory but as a matter of local topographical interest it may be noted that the prior of Warter, Thomas Rooland, who himself had been master of the hospital, was given licence in 1412 to alienate in perpetuity to certain named burgesses, for the sum of £60, a close belonging to the hospital called 'St Giles Croft'. The rents from St Giles Croft field and Keldgate 'leases' later formed a useful proportion of the town's income.

Other hospital foundations included the Trinity Hospital of John de Ake (Aike), a merchant of the town. Established just before the end of the 14th century, this was for a chaplain and 24 poor people. It was built on the Cross Bridge over the Walker Beck near the point of junction of Walkergate and present-day Butcher Row and hence no doubt enjoyed the unusual convenience of water-borne sanitation. Lesser hospitals, additional to St Nicholas' Hospital, included those of St Mary outside the North Bar, St John's in Lairgate, a leper house outside the North Bar and another outside the Keldgate Bar. Almshouses in Wood Lane and in Dead Lane (a narrow lane on the edge of St Mary's graveyard) are also recorded. These smaller houses have left little mark in official records and their existence is mainly attested by occasional notice of gift or bequest, but the lack of historical evidence cannot be regarded as a measure of unimportance to the medieval town community. The medieval hospital-almshouse coped with obvious human needs: its foundation and continued support by the faithful reflected not only the belief that for the giver good works here below substantially enhanced the possibility of eternal salvation hereafter, but also basic human qualities of kindliness and charity of donor and testator alike towards their less fortunate townsmen.

---

* The site now occupied by Lairgate Hall.

4. TUDOR REFORMATION AND STUART RESTORATION

The historian quite rightly regards the middle years of the 16th century as a watershed in English history. But what is today blandly labelled 'The Reformation' was, to the men of the time, a revolution. To Beverley, as elsewhere, royal policy after 1530 brought cataclysmic change and had immediate devitalising effect and long-term consequence for the town. This period not only saw the town as a storm centre of the widespread unrest of the Pilgrimage of Grace, the spoliation of the two friaries, the sequestration of chantry and hospital lands but, most dramatic of all, with Crown appropriation of its properties and endowments, the reduction of the Minster collegiate church to the humble status of a parish church. Furthermore, the Archbishop's relinquishment to the Crown in 1543 of his lordship of Beverley was not merely coincident with renewed royal interest in Hull as a northern military base, but may be interpreted in some measure as evidence of Henry VIII's determination to maintain a more direct control in the strategically sensitive area after the debacle of the Pilgrimage of Grace. The strengthening of the port by the building of additional fortifications increased Hull's regional influence in a number of ways: Beverley was to be seriously affected by such change.

Beverley's economic decline continued. With certain other towns it was named in an Act of 1535 as being one where there were many houses 'in greate ruin and decaye and specially in the pryncipalle and chief stretes', a comprehensive statement which, in Beverley's own case, conflicts somewhat with the impression given by John Leland at about the same time. But half a century later the evidence is far more precise. In 1599 a royal discharge to the town according it release from certain tax obligations, referred to it as being 'an antient towne and heretofore verie ritche and populous' but which, by then, had become so poor that it contained no fewer than 400 decayed and uninhabited tenements. But such poverty is explicable, for long before 1600 the important medieval Yorkshire centres of cloth manufacture of Beverley and York had to yield their pre-eminence to Leeds, Halifax and Wakefield.

Locally, Beverley had to reckon with the all-pervading influence of the Percies at nearby Leconfield and, in the age of the over-mighty subject, the townsmen were inevitably involved in Percy/Lancastrian politics. Mid-15th-century borough records attest the close relationship between the burgesses and their powerful patrons, and in 1461 a contingent of Beverley men, fortified apparently with a shillingsworth of wine 'for the road', went off to fight at Towton where Henry Percy, the third Earl, and his brother Richard were slain in what was the bloodiest battle of the Wars of the Roses. Henry Percy, son of the third Earl, after imprisonment in the Tower, was restored to his earldom in 1470 and 15 years later saved his skin by deserting Richard III at Bosworth Field. He was murdered at Cocklodge, near Thirsk, in 1489 and his identification with Beverley is underlined by his elaborate and expensive funeral at the Minster, and the Percy Chapel built to accommodate his remains. His son, Henry Algernon, 'the Magnificent', kept splendid court at Leconfield and Wressle, lived to see his son and heir an unsuccessful suitor for the hand of Anne Boleyn, but not long enough, fortunately, to see Thomas, his second son, executed at Tyburn for the part he played in the Pilgrimage of Grace rebellion. As far as Beverley was concerned, independence of the powerful Earls Percy was impossible. Borough accounts record the various *curialitates* [gratuities] dispensed to Percy retainers and servants when the Governors were entertained at Leconfield, and the town's reciprocal gifts to its Percy patron. The tangled skein of influence, patronage and retainer rivalries can never be unravelled but c.1528 there is a hint of the local political setting when, for example, Wolsey, as Archbishop of York (and therefore as Lord of Beverley), was complaining that his own nominee as Town Clerk had been dismissed by Percy partisans in the town. The bailiff of the provost had been beaten up because of his apparent refusal to avoid the company of the unfortunate victims: and yet Henry Percy, the sixth Earl, had once been a page in Wolsey's household.

Smaller men also fished in troubled waters when opportunity offered. The Ellerkers of Risby, for instance, had little reason to wish to pray for the well-being of the archbishop Lord of Beverley. In 1516 Sir Ralph Ellerker, who had been indulging himself in the pleasures of the chase in the archiepiscopal park (a merry local custom with long tradition behind it), was compelled by Cardinal Archbishop Wolsey formally to acknowledge his sins which also included similar sporting activities in the Archbishop's preserves at Sherburn and Cawood. He also had to admit responsibility for the kidnapping of George Millet, the keeper of Beverley Parks, and for that unfortunate servant's imprisonment at Cottingham. In 1534 Ellerker went a stage further and took a house in Beverley, thereby establishing what may be termed a burgess property qualification: on the strength of this, he got himself elected a town governor. Apparently his year of office was much to his liking and, despite the rule that a governor was not immediately eligible for a second term, he secured his own re-election and those of 7 other retiring governors by the eminently simple device of kidnapping 14 of the opposition leaders, general strong-arm tactics and 'terryball wordes, thretenynges and other opprobryous wordes not convenyent to be put in writing' against any who opposed him.

Archbishop Edward Lee declared the election null and void and nominated an archiepiscopal commission of 'divers discreet gentlemen', mainly Justices of the Peace, to investigate the whole circumstances. The discreet commission arrived in Beverley but was unable to carry out its inquiries as Sir Ralph had a small army of 140 well-armed men at his back and made his own intentions in the matter only too clear. Meanwhile, Sir

Ralph, his son-in-law, Oswin Ogle, and their gang mocked the authority of the Archbishop by poaching in Beverley Parks and taking a buck and 300 deer. The Archbishop's Beverley problems were by no means wholly resolved by an order in Star Chamber putting an end to Sir Ralph Ellerker's frolics and by an injunction laid on all parties designed to ensure the 'common welth and quyetnes of the sayde towne'. There was further trouble over the election of governors in 1536: with this election, it would seem, Ellerker had no obvious personal concern. But Beverley was in an unsettled state and it is not difficult to understand why the town played an important part in the Pilgrimage of Grace: as Archbishop Lee pithily commented, 'There were many light heads in Beverley' at this time.

★ ★ ★

In the so-called Priest's Room at the east end of St Mary's church there survives a piece of 16th-century oak which at one time had been reused in a later canopied pew. It bears a carved commemorative inscription beseeching the Almighty to have mercy on the souls of the men, women and children killed 'at the faulyng of thys Scherc' [church] on 29 April 1520, and on those who had been or would be parties to its rising-up again'. The tragedy came on the third Sunday after Easter that year and, although this and other extant contemporary references do not specify the nature of the disaster, the architectural evidence today makes it clear that it was the tower which fell: presumably it collapsed westwards over the nave. It needs little imagination to appreciate what this would mean in terms of loss of life since the surviving inscription clearly infers that the tragedy occurred in service time.

The rebuilding of the greater part of the church was obviously necessary and commemorative plaques along the north arcade of the nave testify in this regard to the respective efforts of John Crossley and his wife Joan, the minstrels and the 'good wives'. But there were others who helped and the oak inscription, for example, records specifically the generosity of Sir Richard Rokeby and Joan, his wife. Rokeby at this time was Wolsey's comptroller of the household. The gift of a new font in 1530 by William Leryfaxe, draper, and his wife, suggests both a terminal date for the work of restoration as well as the possibility that the earlier font had been damaged or destroyed. If such were the case, then it is likely that the west end of the nave also suffered seriously in the catastrophe. Externally today, the noble church, with slight modifications, is as the Tudor masons restored it. Because they salvaged what they could in order to rebuild, the visitor can be pleasingly perplexed by the juxtaposition and variety of examples of medieval building style: therein lies much of the charm of this splendid parish church.

★ ★ ★

Henry VIII's attack on the monasteries came in 1536. Following official valuation of ecclesiastical and monastic revenues in 1535, the blow – not entirely without precedent – fell on the smaller houses. Under the Act of

1536, the preamble of which sought to justify such action by evidence of 'manifest sin, vicious, carnal and abominable living', commissioners set to work to implement royal policy. But reaction was swift. Early in October that year rebellion broke out at Louth in Lincolnshire and spread rapidly. It was not merely an expression of widespread objection to the suppression of these smaller monasteries, sympathy with the dispersed monks and nuns or disgust at the indecency and coarseness of the visiting commissioners and their gangs of attendant jackals, but the fear, too, that parish churches were also on the royal agenda. These and other grievances – some real, others imaginary – gave seasoning to the revolt. The rebellion spread in Lincolnshire like a prairie fire, articles were drawn up presenting the King with certain demands – the last and most important being a pardon for all participants – and, while the King's reply to his 'rude commons of one shire and that one of the most brute and beastly of the whole realm and of least experience' was being awaited, the Lincolnshire rebels, having little effective leadership and less discipline, began to slip away. Henry, of course, had his due revenge and some 50 ringleaders were executed.

But, as the rebellion in Lincolnshire weakened, revolt erupted in the north with Beverley as a focal point in eastern Yorkshire. Robert Aske of Aughton, a lawyer and a somewhat enigmatic figure, emerged, not as the commander-in-chief of an army bent on civil war, but as the leader of commons who sought to represent to the king the shortcomings of royal advisers. William Stapleton of Wighill, another lawyer and himself a friend of Aske, became Captain of the Beverley host. Christopher Stapleton, the head of the Stapleton family, and his wife were staying at the Beverley Grey Friars and William was there with them. With the Lincolnshire rebellion barely a week old, the town was in a state of excitement and on 8 October Beverley men mustered on Westwood Low Green. Christopher, a sick man and fearful of the upset, ordered his family to stay indoors except 'one simple fellow not of estimation called George Bell' who was sent into the Market Place to report what was happening. But Christopher's wife, Elizabeth (the daughter of Sir John Neville of Liversedge), was a woman of different calibre and as the people of Beverley, in militant mood, streamed past on their way to the Westwood – 'the wife of the said Christopher went forth and stood in a close where a great number of them were come of the other side of the hedge and she saying "God's blessing have ye" and "Speed ye well in your good purpose". Then said they, "Where is your husband and his folks that he cometh not as others doeth?" and she said, "They may be in the Friars – go pull them out by the heads."' Mistress Stapleton's intransigence not only indicated her own enthusiastic support of the commons of Beverley but explains why the sickly Christopher, on hearing what had happened, 'wished himself out of this world'.

Following a muster at Market Weighton hill it was agreed that Aske should march on York and Stapleton on Hull. Both places capitulated and, in this third week of the October rebellion, there were further risings throughout the north. But by the end of the month negotiations at Doncaster had resulted in an armistice, a dispersal of both armies and a royal invitation to Aske to present himself at court. Aske spent Christmas in London and was apparently well received by the King. Early in January he was back in the East Riding and able to report to a meeting at Beverley the results of a successful London mission. But Aske had returned to a north seething with rumours that Henry was only temporising while royal force was being organised in strength. Then came the final crisis. In mid-January John Hallam of Cawkeld near Watton ('so fierce and cruel a man among his neighbours that no man durst disobey him'), and Sir Francis Bigod of Settrington made attempts on Hull and Scarborough. As far as the King was concerned, the point of no return had now been reached. Aske was decoyed to London and other leaders were tried and executed. Early in July, Aske too met his fate at Clifford's Tower in York. William Stapleton was fortunate – he was not numbered among Henry's sacrificial victims. It has been said that posterity passes harsh judgement on the failed rebel. Aske paid the penalty of rebellion with his life at the hands of a king he trusted too well and whom he would gladly have served. The church tower of Aughton, despite the problem of the inscription on its south face, remains an Aske memorial of these fateful years.*

In East Riding of Yorkshire Archives Services is a copy of the general pardon granted by Henry when the blood-letting was over. The concluding paragraph of the pardon exempted from royal mercy the names of those on an annexed schedule: the first names on the list of 21 who were to be 'utterly excepted and forprised oute of this pardon' are those of Richard Wilson and William Woodmansey of Beverley.

After the Pilgrimage of Grace the blow fell upon the rest of the monasteries and Beverley's two friaries were sacrificed with them. The seven-acre site of the Grey Friars outside the Keldgate Bar was surrendered on 25 February, 1539, to Richard Ingworth, Bishop of Dover, who had been appointed King's Visitor for the suppression of the houses of mendicant friars in England and Wales. The following day Ingworth received the surrender of the Dominican friary. The church plate of both found its way into the royal treasury. The Dominicans' Beverley property came into the hands of Richard Fayrecliff who, as tenant, paid 20 shillings a year rent for it but, with other church lands, the site and surviving buildings were sold in 1544 to John Pope and Anthony Foster of London. In the early 18th century the property belonged to Sir Michael Warton and in due course was bought by the Earls of Yarborough who built up extensive interests in and around Beverley. Early last century the Yarboroughs began to dispose of their Beverley estates and, as a result, in 1826, Richard Whiteing of Beverley Parks became the owner of the Friary: the Whiteing family

---

* Pevsner gives the translation, 'Christopher the second son of Sir Robert Aske ought not to forget the year 1536', a probable reference to the Pilgrimage of Grace.

maintained an interest in the property until it was sold to Messrs. Armstrong Patents Ltd, in 1961 for industrial development.

But in Beverley worse was to come. The onslaught on all types of chantry foundation which began almost too quietly in the last years of Henry VIII's reign reached hurricane force with the protectorate of the Duke of Somerset following the accession of the young Edward VI in 1547. Essentially it was a logical continuance of anti-monastic policy which was given renewed energy by developing Protestantism with its hostility to the doctrine of purgatory and masses for the dead. The Act of 1545, prompted in some measure by financial needs arising from the war with France, vested chantry lands in the King for the term of his life and authorised the appointment of commissioners to inquire into chantry endowments. Relatively little was done immediately but in 1547, under the 'Act whereby certain chantries, colleges, free chapels and possessions of the same be given to the King's Majesty', chantry endowments were sequestrated by the Crown, and collegiate foundations like Beverley Minster were also declared dissolved, their properties, goods and wealth being forfeited to the King. There can be no doubt that in view of the royal order of 1541 the shrine of St John had already been taken down and it is probable too that, about this time, the reputed relics and associated objects were placed in the nave vault where they are today.

In consequence of this revolutionary change, Beverley Minster lost its collegiate status and on Easter Day 1548 became a parish church serving a town parish of St Martin and a parish of St John the Evangelist co-extensive with the ancient liberties. Out of the endowments thus appropriated pensions were paid to the unbeneficed dispossessed, Reginald Lee, for example, the last of the provosts of Beverley, being granted an annual pension of £50. But reconstitution of the Minster as a parish church involved the creation of a new benefice (a vicarage valued at £13. 6s. 8d. per annum) with provision for three curacies worth £8 each. The first vicar of the Minster, Thomas Mitchell, was a former vicar choral of the collegiate church, was 52 years old and is noted as being 'indifferently larned' – a description more complimentary then than it would be today. The curates were Thomas Dringe, also a former vicar choral, Anthony Collinson, late chantry priest of St Katherine's chantry, and William Jeffrey, a former priest of the chantry of the Holy Trinity. Collinson seems to have died at or about this time and John Atkinson (also a priest of St Katherine's chantry) succeeded him.

With so much more Crown land available for lease or sale after this second sequestration within a decade, speculators and vultures foregathered for the pickings. Strictly legal, of course, though his activities were, the arch-villain as far as Beverley Minster lands were concerned was Michael Stanhope. His father, Sir Edward Stanhope, had been knighted by Henry VII on Blackfield Heath for signal service to the Tudor cause: the son followed in his father's footsteps and in 1542 was appointed deputy-governor of Hull, succeeding to the governorship on the death, in 1548, of his immediate superior, Sir Richard Long. Stanhope had done well already out of monastic spoils and particularly so in respect of the two Nottinghamshire priories of Lenton and Shelford. After 1547, by purchase or lease, he managed to come into possession of considerable chantry properties in East Yorkshire including those of the ancient hospital of St Mary Magdalene at Killingwoldgraves. The Minster prebendal lands of St Michael and St Andrew fell into his lap and then, in association with John Bellow, another enthusiastic land-jobber, he acquired all the prebendal houses round the Minster, the houses of the four officers of the Chapter and much else. His easy success, no doubt, may be explained by family influence; his half-sister Anne was the wife of the Protector, Edward Seymour, Duke of Somerset.

It was Stanhope who was responsible in 1550 for the demolition of the octagonal chapter house north of the choir, the 'Chapel of Our Lady' and the charnel house at the south-west corner of the nave. Over this charnel was the chapel of St Martin, architectural indications of which remain today. The materials were sold off for £100, the lead from the roofs being bought by John Packer, a Hull merchant. Two years before this, and in association with Bellow, Stanhope had been pillaging the Hall Garth, the ruined manor house of the archbishops at Beverley to the south of the Minster, in order to build a hunting lodge in Beverley Parks. Setting aside the legal niceties of the situation, it would not be unfair to label Stanhope as the arch despoiler of the Minster. He did not live long to enjoy his gains: with Somerset he was charged with conspiracy to assassinate the Duke of Northumberland and was executed in 1552.

Government confiscation of the endowments of the former collegiate church presented the town with two urgent problems – the question of the future maintenance of the fabric and the continuance of the Minster's grammar school. In 1552 – or it may have been a little earlier as the petition is undated – and on the grounds that 'the said churche is veray greate and ruinuse' the burgesses sought the grant of the estates which had financed the medieval Minster's 'Office of Works'. This 'Office' had been responsible for the upkeep of the fabric and its value at the dissolution was assessed at £68. 1s. 0d. Furthermore, it was represented to the Crown that with a population of some 5,000, Beverley had a 'grate numbre of youthe', some of whom were 'apt and meet to be brought up in learning'.

Supplication for financial aid for maintenance of the Minster fabric was successful and the town's twelve Governors became the trustees of lands formerly attached to the old Office of Works, and valued at approximately £54 a year: later, in 1579, there was a further grant from the Crown. These 'Minster Estates' formed the nucleus of what ultimately became known as the Minster Old Fund, and until the Municipal Corporations Act of 1835 the Corporation continued as trustees. Without these lands and properties Beverley Minster's fate may well have been that of Howden's, where today

the glorious 14th-century choir lies in lamentable ruin.

The medieval Minster's grammar school, as later, no doubt occupied a site in the south-west area of the churchyard. The school itself was of ancient foundation and evidence suggests an existence as early as c.1100 although it may even have had its beginnings in the time of Bishop John. The greatest of its alumni was undoubtedly John Fisher, the saintly bishop of Rochester, who did not live to see the radical changes of the middle years of the 16th century – he died on the scaffold on Tower Hill in 1535 for his principled opposition to Henry VIII and because, unlike others, he refused to trim his sails to wind of political circumstance. No financial provision for the Minster grammar school was made by the Crown out of the Minster estates. The school was taken over by the Corporation, which thereby ensured its continuity at a major crisis in its long history. Until 1816, when it was moved to nearby Keldgate, Beverley and East Riding youth 'apt and meet for learning' continued to be educated in the shadow of the Minster church.

The dissolution of the collegiate church clearly had serious consequences for the town for, at one fell blow, the Chantries Act of 1547 effectively destroyed its importance as an ecclesiastical centre and that of the Minster church itself as a sub-cathedral of the diocese of York. It is impossible to assess what all this meant in simple economic terms. But the revolution of the Reformation also meant that no longer was the town and its liberties a sanctified reception area for criminal elements. Traditionally since the days of Athelstan the collegiate church had enjoyed rights of chartered sanctuary. The criminal was given protection for 30 days following his formal oath-taking to be of good behaviour and to undertake certain simple obligations. But, unlike a fugitive seeking sanctuary in an ordinary church, he was not required to abjure the realm: consequently the town at one time or another must have harboured several of these grithmen as they were called. Rights of sanctuary were gradually whittled down by Tudor statute until in 1540 all sanctuaries were abolished except certain places and churches listed in the Act – and Beverley was not one of them: in any case even these, in respect of certain types of major crime, were excluded from the right of according protection.

Beverley's sanctuary register for the period c.1478-1539 is extant and contains the names of 469 self-acknowledged criminals and debtors. Over a closely comparable 60-year period (1464-1524) 247 sanctuary seekers were registered at Durham, a comparison which suggests that by the 15th century either St John had the edge on St Cuthbert, or, more likely, that Beverley was, geographically, more convenient for the criminal classes. Yet, when measured against the turbulence of 15th- and 16th-century society, Beverley's average yearly intake over this period of seven or eight grithmen does not seem unduly excessive: not all necessarily stayed in the town.

★ ★ ★

The third great Act of spoliation against the church came towards the end of the reign of Edward VI. In the official view, doctrinal change and the new forms and patterns of church service rendered superfluous much of the plate, vestments and valuables in parish church and cathedral alike. Accordingly, church inventories were ordered to be made under the general supervision of commissioners appointed for each shire and the final seizure of surplus goods came early in 1553: one chalice per parish church, two for a cathedral or large church and a reasonable stock of linen were to be left but copes, altar cloths, ornaments and metal goods (except bells) were to be sold off for the benefit of the poor. Although the inventory for Beverley St Mary's is mutilated, it is clear, for example, that the church had a good collection of copes, including one of 'white damask with birds and beasts'. St Nicholas' church, which could then boast of three bells in the tower, was also reasonably well provided with vestments. As would be expected, the Minster was also well supplied and *inter alia* 'a pair of great organs' and six bells are recorded. The death of Edward VI and the accession of Mary naturally resulted in a volte-face in this policy of official theft. The small amount of plate which was still intact was, for the most part, returned but naturally what had already been melted down was retained. None of the surviving Beverley church plate dates from before the Reformation period except a medieval latten coffin chalice belonging to the Minster. This was presented to the church last century and is believed to have been found in a grave in the Minster: it had once formed part of the collection of the antiquarian Gillyat Sumner of Woodmansey.

Despite the Catholic reaction of Mary's short reign and the activity of the church courts, Protestant opinion in Beverley was by no means stifled. Thomas Mitchell, the vicar of the Minster, apparently did not find it so difficult to play the role of a minor vicar of Bray and proved an acceptable agent for superintending acts of public penance imposed on local offenders. In 1556 John Bonsaye confessed to giving public utterance to Protestant views on the doctrine of transubstantiation and his friend John Peesgrave, a fuller, was found to have three heretical and seditious books in his possession. Both offenders were assigned appropriate penance and, on completion of Peesgrave's sentence, Mitchell was deputed to supervise the public burning of the offending literature at the Market Cross. This particular operation must have been effectively carried out for it cost the Corporation no less than fourpence for the necessary faggots. The titles of these literary works are known and provide interesting commentary themselves on the 'heretical' literature of the period, as well as the apparent literacy of ordinary laymen. Two years before this, Richard Bigott had been accused of railing against the Holy Sacrament and gathering together like-minded 'protestants' in his house. About the same time seven other Beverlonians – most of them leading townsmen – were in similar trouble. With Bigott they were ordered to purge themselves by the oaths of their neighbours and no doubt did not find this too difficult. Clearly the town was restive, but unlike Richard Snell of Bedale, who was burnt at the stake in Richmond Market Place in 1558, no East Riding heretic suffered a similar fate at any auto-da-fé in the shadow of Beverley's Market Cross. One suspects that in the capital of the East Riding the ecclesiastical revolution of the reign of Edward VI was not unwelcome.

★   ★   ★

In the autumn of 1541 Henry's 'progress' into the northern parts of his kingdom – designedly part of the royal policy of pacification after the troubles of the Pilgrimage of Grace – brought him to Beverley after the court had made an overnight stop at Leconfield Castle en route to Hull. Beverley had already presented the King with £10 as a 'benevolence' and the various incidental and expected payments to members of the royal entourage at this time made undue demands on town resources. But the King's visit was to have unexpected results. The royal decision at the time to make Hull 'mighty strong' led to the building of substantial additional tower fortifications on the Drypool side of the river: these were linked to the western defences by Hull's first North Bridge, which replaced an ancient ferry. This bridge had a moveable central leaf or trap to allow ships to pass through with masts erect. Henceforth, Hull's effective control of shipping along the river became a matter of increasing concern to Beverley shipmen and other river traders, and particularly so when Hull 'closed and made up the said leaf or trap', thereby making it impossible for vessels to pass the bridge with masts unstepped. In an age when road communications were poor, Beverley's river link with the Humber was all-important.

Together with other interested parties the town complained to the Crown in 1559 and, as was usual in such cases, the Privy Council nominated arbitrators. The case was investigated and an 'award' made.

Hull was ordered to 'disclose' the bridge and allow free passage: Beverley was to contribute towards the remedial operation. In addition, the preparatory legal business at Hull, York and London proved expensive for the town. This whole question of free navigation of the River Hull was complicated by the fact that, while Hull acknowledged the right of free passage for Beverley ships along the natural river, the Hull aldermen maintained, not without legal justification, that the low reach of the river above its confluence with the Humber was a new cut or channel to which Beverley's claims could not apply. The bridge long continued to be a matter of irritation. Even as late as 1788, following a rebuilding of the North Bridge, Beverley was still concerned about river traders' rights of passage and the tolls Hull was demanding. The whole problem was, of course, progressively worsened by increasing shipping congestion in Hull's haven.

★ ★ ★

Letters Patent from Elizabeth in 1573 'incorporated' the borough, according it the right to have a mayor, a recorder, two Members of Parliament and certain other privileges. A significant change was that, by its terms, a permanent self-perpetuating body of 13 ruling governors was established (one governor serving as mayor) with the loosely phrased proviso that the burgesses as a whole could be joined with the mayor and governors to 'hear, refer, consult and decree'. This development of an oligarchic conciliar system contrasted with the more democratic one it superseded: at the same time, it helped towards a continuity of rule which was formerly lacking. By 1600 the pattern of town rule had become fixed – a permanent body of 13 governors or aldermen, 'assistant' to which was an annually elected group of 13 'capital burgesses' who were chosen by the burgesses at large from a list of 26 nominated by the governors. This borough constitution effectively put the responsibility of rule in the hands of the governors but, at the same time, the group of associated capital burgesses provided a useful link between the governors and commonalty and in practice was not without its own effectiveness. With slight modification (and threatened upset at the Restoration) this pattern lasted until municipal reform came in 1835.

Town government, of course, was not without its brighter moments and when Corporation policy cut across individual burgess interests reaction could be brisk. In 1602 there was upset at the election of the mayor and a riot was followed by two or three gaol sentences: apparently some burgesses wished to elect as mayor one Rydley, who was not a governor. There were even more rumbustious scenes in 1610 when the mayor and his brethren were physically assaulted and a rescue made of Marmaduke Attmar who had been taken into custody. Naturally, many cases of 'contemptius speatches' and vulgar abuse of the Corporation went unrecorded but in 1604 the mayor and his fellow justices decided to commit Richard Wrightson and David Cotterill to gaol to cool off for

The White Horse ('Nellie's'), Hengate, has 17th-century origins.

giving utterance to 'undecent' speeches According to the record, Wrightson had merely expressed the opinion that the governors ought to be hanged and Cotterill had indelicately wished that the tongues of some of the members of the Corporation ought to be on a string – innocuous maybe, but presumably the scribe decided that as far as the record was concerned any linguistic embellishments were not 'convenient to be put into writing'.

★ ★ ★

It cannot be said that in the 16th century standards of public health and sanitation were any higher than those of a century before. Garbage and house filth in the streets, wandering dogs and rooting pigs, 'gutters' left uncleansed and a virtual lack of environmental consciousness only paralleled in attitude by the litter lout today – this is the picture which stands out from the record. Disease of one sort or another was doubtless always present, but in 1604, when both York and Hull were also badly affected, the town suffered a vicious outbreak of plague. The usual precautions were taken, including a constantly maintained watch by householders in respective wards. The Minster registers alone for the period August 1604 - June 1605 record no fewer than 200 burials – four times the average. Of these, 148 were recorded as being deaths *per pestum* and closer analysis shows that it was the town parish of St Martin which suffered and not the outlying hamlets within the parish of St John.

In June, 1610, the pestilence struck again and the parish clerk of St Mary's registered the burial that month of 23 people who had died from plague 'besides fortie that was shufled into graves without any reading over them at all' – compelling evidence of a crisis situation. No one was to visit any market or fair without leave of the mayor, there was the heavy penalty of 40 shillings for every period of six hours the disease remained unnotified (how the regulation worked in practice is unrecorded) and arrangements were made for the relief of the sick poor. The Trinities was used as a pest house or isolation centre and, in more modern times, the finding of graves in the vicinity of the railway station no doubt attests the use of this area as a plague burial ground. But, somewhat surprisingly, and despite its close proximity to the Humber port, Beverley seems to have escaped infection when Hull suffered a massive visitation between 1635 and 1638 and nearly 3,000 people died. Beverley's quarantine regulations at this time were naturally rigid and included the prohibition of any 'publique' meetings and gatherings of more than ten people 'upon womens occasions as child-bearings or Christninges'.

Beverley's turn came again in 1665 when both Hull and York escaped. Infection on this occasion may have been brought into the town by London merchants who were regular visitors to Beverley's annual Rogationtide fair. In this epidemic there were even more stringent control regulations. The outbreak seems to have been particularly vicious in the immediate vicinity of the Minster and all dogs and cats in the Wednesday Market-Highgate-Eastgate area were ordered to be killed forthwith. Any statistical assessment of the impact upon the town of this – Beverley's last infection by plague – is impossible: like the great cholera epidemics of the 19th century no doubt it helped in some degree towards the beginnings of increased awareness of a need for urban environmental improvement.

But plague was not the only misery of these middle years of the 17th century. Unlike Hull and York, Beverley was an open town and suffered when civil war broke out in 1642. It came within the orbital influence of the major military prize of Hull, and thus paid the penalty for having no effective defence works when Royalist operations were mounted against the Parliamentary stronghold. On 23 April 1642, Sir John Hotham, the Parliamentary governor of Hull, denied Charles I entrance to the town when the young Prince James, Duke of York, was being entertained by the Brethren of Hull Trinity House. Together with the Prince, Charles returned to Beverley and stayed overnight at the house of Lady Gee, near the North Bar. From Beverley he sent two heralds back to Hull to demand the town's surrender, which was refused. A few weeks later Hull was subjected to its first siege and, after months of heart searching, Hotham switched his allegiance from Parliament to King. He realised he was justifiably suspect by Parliament and, following action taken to arrest him early on 29 June 1643, he escaped from Hull, hoping to reach the comparative security of his fortified manor house at Scorborough; he tried

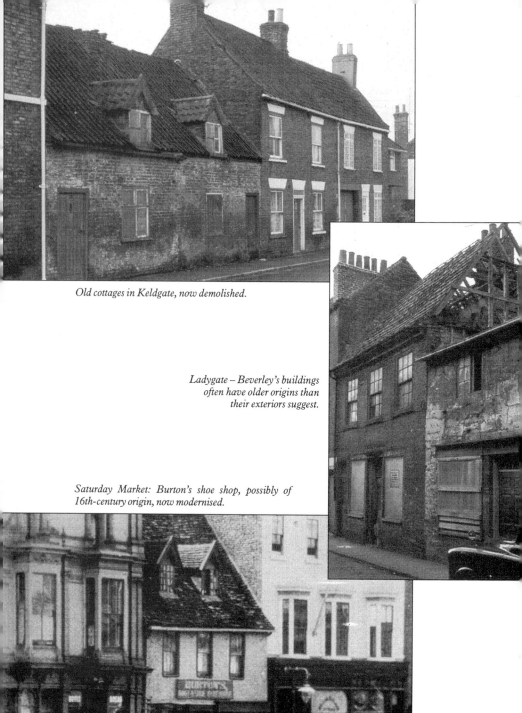

Old cottages in Keldgate, now demolished.

Ladygate – Beverley's buildings often have older origins than their exteriors suggest.

Saturday Market: Burton's shoe shop, possibly of 16th-century origin, now modernised.

unsuccessfully to cross the River Hull at Stoneferry and again at Wawne and then galloped determinedly into Beverley to find troops drawn up on morning parade. With unusual decision and quickness of mind he rode to their front and commanded them to follow him. But the hunt was up. A cavalcade of troops under the command of Matthew Boynton clarified the position for the surprised Beverley contingent. Even then, Hotham tried to make his escape but was knocked off his horse by one of Boynton's troopers. Bruised and cut, he was taken back to Hull and with his son was shipped off to London. Eighteen months later, on Tower Hill, father and son paid the penalty of treachery.

At the time of Hotham's capture, Parliament's forces were trounced at the Battle of Adwalton Moor, near Bradford: the defeated remnants made for Hull as being virtually the only Parliamentary stronghold left in the north. After an unwise delay, the royalist Marquis of Newcastle prepared to besiege Hull and by the end of August 1643 was moving against the Parliamentary garrison there with some 12,000 foot and 4,000 horse. Meanwhile, Sir Thomas Fairfax, who had been ravaging as far west from Hull as Stamford Bridge, was holding Beverley with some 1,800 foot and 20 troops of horse. Beverley was, of course, militarily untenable and Fairfax sought permission to fall back on Hull. To cover withdrawal of his infantry, many of them 'freshwater soldiers', as a contemporary called them, he had to use his cavalry in a series of brisk delaying actions. Hence, the fighting in and around Beverley was vicious, fierce and bloody and the town was cruelly plundered 'in a most tyrannous way'. The Royalist siege of Hull failed and, as the King's troops withdrew to York through Beverley, the town was again subjected to a brutal pillage: it is probably understandable that for exactly two years after October 1642 there is no record of meetings of the Corporation. But Nicholas Pearson, the schoolmaster-parish clerk of St Mary's (1636-53), has left in his parish register, in a partial cryptogram which would deceive no 17th-century intelligence officer, a pithy record of these years of strife.

Parliamentary Hull's regional influence was strong but not strong enough to negate or eradicate the Royalist element in Beverley. From 1642-44 Beverley had a Royalist mayor in Robert Manbie but, on the evidence, it was clearly factional strife in the town which ultimately prompted His Worship to collect up the Borough mace, plate, and some Corporation and other moneys and decamp with the spoil to the Royalist headquarters at York. But Manbie had backed the wrong horse, and a month after the Royalist disaster at Marston Moor the Parliamentary standing committee at York took appropriate steps to ensure that Manbie was discharged from his corporate offices of mayor and governor.

As elsewhere, well-heeled Royalists in the town paid heavily for 'delinquency' and had to compound for their estates. Among them were the Warton and Gee families but lesser-known local Royalists, such as Robert Leeds and John Taylor of Molescroft, also suffered for their faithful adherence to the Stuart cause.

5. IMPROVEMENT AND RENEWAL 1660-1835

On her way to visit her relative, Sir Griffith Boynton of Burton Agnes, that spirited and courageous traveller Celia Fiennes visited Beverley in 1697. The town impressed her – it was 'very fine for its size' and preferable to any other town she had seen except Nottingham. The buildings were 'new and pretty lofty' and the streets 'well pitch'd'. She found the Minster impressive, and fish – for Mistress Fiennes had a strong streak of gastronomic awareness – was plentiful and cheap. In fact, before the end of the 17th century, Beverley had made a good recovery from the trials and troubles of civil war, and there is evidence that by 1688 a family like the unfortunate Wartons, for example, had more than recouped its fortunes. Rebuilding reflected increasing wealth deriving not only from trade generally but from more prosperous farming and improved estate management, which made it possible for more than one neighbouring country squire to have his Beverley town house. Before the end of the 17th century John Burnsall, the Hull antiquarian, noted that many gentry resided in Beverley. As Tate Wilkinson was to comment a century on, late 18th-century Beverley was not a town of trade but, like York, was 'chiefly supported by the genteel private families that reside there in continuance'.

Market Cross.

Between the Restoration and 1800 improvement of the town was considerable – evidence of a growing civic and communal pride. Early in 1707, for instance, the old Market Cross was seriously damaged: according to a tradition recorded in 1829 by George Oliver, Beverley's historian, it was a large structure and big enough for a carriage to pass through. But despite adverse economic conditions, the Corporation immediately launched a public subscription which, in the delicious phraseology of the new chamber clerk, Daniel Carver, was to be 'towards the building of a new cross in Saturday Market where the present cross, lately demolished, now stands'. The scheme languished somewhat but, with financial help from Sir Charles Hotham and Sir Michael Warton, the two Members of Parliament, the work, begun in 1711 was finished in 1714. The cross was built to the design of Samuel Shelton* of Wakefield. It is worth noting that in 1707 Wakefield, too, got a new Market Cross: the Beverley one was of a similar design. But unlike those of Wakefield, York and Hull, which paid the penalty of later market place improvements, Beverley's cross fortunately still stands, a fair ornament to the town, and architecturally and aesthetically an elegant example of its type and period.

A cross in Wednesday Market was erected in 1723 at the instance of Alderman Henry Jarratt. Unfortunately, it was 'vandalised' in 1755, some of its stepped base being removed. Following improvement in the Wednesday Market area, which included repaving, it was decided to replace it. The Corporation commissioned Edward Rushforth, a local mason, to carry out the work: but the result was an obelisk, not a cross, which adorned Wednesday Market Place until 1881 when it, too, paid the penalty of progress.

The rebuilding of the Town Hall in 1762 by the Corporation produced another building which today is a worthy part of Beverley's Georgian heritage. Archbishop Thurstan's charter (c.1129) had granted the men of Beverley the right to their own 'hanshus' or 'gild house'. Where this building was is not known but, after 1282, the medieval keepers were making use of the 'Byscopdyngs' or Archbishop's Hall in the Market Place, which Archbishop William Wickwane had granted to the burgesses for a nominal annual payment. It is presumed that this was a typical medieval hall over a basement with external access stair. From about 1386, however, the town's keepers were renting the hall of the gild of St John in Walkergate. In 1500 the Borough acquired its own 'town's hall' with the purchase of the 'great messuage' of Edward Mynskyp in the Cross Garths. This cost the town £76. 6s. 8d., plus a pasture known as the Tonge at the east end of the Beck. As a result of this transaction the Corporation came into possession of no fewer than 27 deeds relating to the property in the Cross Garths and dating back to c.1320 – a unique collection of medieval documents of title.

---

* Pevsner names Theophilus Shelton as the designer.

By the early years of the 18th century the old Town Hall had become unsatisfactory and the fact that, in 1756, when winter was coming on, matting had to be bought to line the wall behind the capital burgesses, suggests that standards of conciliar comfort left something to be desired. With a budget surplus and by some saving on Beck maintenance, rebuilding became financially feasible. The project was discussed in the convivial atmosphere of a local hostelry (committee preliminaries which cost the Corporation 32s. in drink and tobacco) and the plans and estimate of William Middleton were accepted. As soon as building operations were imminent, the Corporation, together with civic impedimenta and records, moved to the workhouse in Minstermoorgate, there to await building completion. By November 1762 the work was finished and it was decided to carry out appropriate interior decoration. A contract was made with the Italian stuccoist Giuseppe Cortese, who had worked at Studley Royal and Gilling Castle. Cortese agreed to provide the king's arms, the town's arms and the figure of Justice with other ornaments 'in Plaister or Stukoe' for 40 guineas. Today the visitor to Beverley's Guildhall needs no convincing that the Corporation struck a good bargain. Cortese's plaster-work ceiling in the Court Room is a veritable tour de force and a remarkable essay both in design and execution. The unwitting symbolism of an all-seeing Justice riding the clouds (she is not represented blindfolded as is traditional), in a setting which is used as a magistrates' court as well as a council chamber,* is itself not without a certain appropriateness.

Some furnishings were retained from the older building, including a mayoral dais of 1604, but new furniture was necessary. In 1764 Edmund Foster was commissioned to do some (unspecified) carved work which almost certainly included the present mayoral dais to which Cortese's royal arms forms such a magnificent reredos. William Thompson, 'joyner', made ten 'armed' chairs for 25s. each and six 'common chairs' for 17s. each: these, with subsequent additions, form part of the very fine set of Chippendale-type furniture which the Corporation possessed.

Although in 1782 proposals were made for the addition of 'commodious dining room with other conveniences', plans for facilities for aldermanic and other junketings were not proceeded with. Substantial additions to the 18th-century Guildhall were made in 1832-33 when Charles Mountain the Younger, the Hull architect, was charged with the responsibility for extensions which included the imposing Doric portico, the public gallery, mayor's parlour with adjoining kitchens and the rooms at the front. This project, on the eve of corporate borough reform, cost more than half the town's income of the previous year and was only really made possible by the sale to the East Riding magistrates of the gaol and gaol-keeper's house on the south side of the Guildhall.

It was by no means unknown for the replacement of old Corporation

---

* No longer so used.

property to be effected by the device of a building lease granted to a sitting tenant or an interested third party. In terms of rent the method was not financially productive, but it released the Corporation from the obligation of carrying out the work directly and had the advantage of allowing the individual some say in the type and character of the house he wanted. And, of course, other types of 'improvement' might also usefully form part of such a scheme as was the case in 1728 when James Butler proposed to rebuild the whole front of his house in Vicar Lane and pave the street fronting the property: he was granted a 99-year building lease. But one of the more important rebuilding programmes of this type affected the block of property in the Dings, east of the Market Cross – houses and shops which were probably on the site of the medieval archbishop's hall. This scheme was proposed by an opportunist alderman, John Hoggard, in his mayorality in 1765. Hoggard was granted a 70-year building lease for £19 per annum in respect of seven separate tenements there: according to the record when the lease was sealed, the rent, for some reason, was only to be £10. The obligation laid on Hoggard was that he was to rebuild the

The Court Room, Guildhall, showing the work of Giuseppe Cortese.

properties within three years according to a plan produced. As far as possible the old tiles were to be re-used and the buildings in every respect 'finished as the house formerly built by Mr Thackeray': Thackeray was a linen draper who had had a building lease on his own in the Dings in 1740. Hoggard raised the necessary capital from his father-in-law and by borrowing £200 of Minster moneys. In 1755, also in the Dings, Luke Williamson was allowed to rebuild 'as Mr Thackeray'. This central rebuilding scheme gives some idea of the control which the Corporation exercised over the preservation of building character. In 1809, the Corporation sold off five of its properties in the Dings in order to buy land in Beverley Parks, part of the Earl of Yarborough's estates. In 1824 the 'Hoggard' houses were also sold on the expiration of the 70-year lease which had been granted to the alderman.

Not all Corporation property rebuilding was effected by such a method. The charming wisteria-clad Newbegin Bar House, at the west end of Newbegin, for instance, was built by direct contract between the Corporation and a local builder, William Wrightson, according to the proposals of Francis Best, who became the Corporation's first lessee. The contract was dated 21 March 1745. The agreement additionally specified that the house was to be painted 'three times over', certain rooms were to be papered, a pump provided, the pump yard was to be paved with cobbles and two 'dung holes' made: the total cost was £315. In 1748, and presumably at Best's request, the Corporation agreed to build a shell over the 'fore door' of the house, the tenant to pay an annual rent of one shilling for every pound the Corporation spent in making the adornment, which unfortunately no longer survives.

In the second half of the 18th century, William Middleton, the builder of the Guildhall, did much building and rebuilding for the Corporation: the financing of his many activities as a builder/architect in Beverley and district was no doubt made easier by his 40-years' retention, as executor, of the substantial legacy of Mrs Ann Wride. In 1793 he and his son John were responsible for the two houses immediately to the east of the North Bar, together with the pedestrian throughwalk at the side of the gateway: it is some measure of the rise in building costs that by this time the Middletons' estimate for such a project was £1,350. The making of the pedestrian way interestingly correlated with contemporary plans for the laying out of New Walk, outside the Bar.

As trustees of the Minster's estates the Corporation in 1703-4 was also concerned with the reconstruction and rebuilding of what is now the Old Minster Vicarage in Minster Yard North. Although no record is apparently extant to substantiate it, there is a strong local tradition that this gracious house, with its charming walled garden, occupies the site of the house of the medieval Minster provosts.

Although the Corporation's responsibility for building and renewal was by no means small, by far the greater amount of domestic building in

18th-century Beverley was the result of private enterprise. As Alderman Matthew Ashmole wrote, c.1694, echoing John Burnsall's comments, the air and situation of Beverley 'occasioned many gentlemen to settle here' and the architecture of the town reflected the fact. In 1698 Yarborough and Rosamund Constable laid out £300 for the building of what was, possibly, their house in Keldgate: in 1709 Mr Henry Spendlove was given permission to raise the pavement along the frontage of his 'new built' house in Hengate and there is little doubt that the magnificent house in Newbegin, once the home of Warton Warton and now represented by numbers 14 and 15, dates back to c.1700 or a little earlier.

But the most spectacular example of what may be described as private environmental planning and house building in early Georgian Beverley was the Eastgate scheme of Sir Charles Hotham, fourth Baronet, one of the two Members of Parliament for the Borough. From 1713 Hotham began a policy of property consolidation on both sides of Eastgate and Colin Campbell was the architect to whose plan, later published in Campbell's *Vitruvius Britannicus*, the house was ultimately built. This house occupied a site on the east side of Eastgate to the south of its junction with Trinity Lane. Although in medieval times local shortage of good quality building stone had given a fillip to the development of brickmaking in Beverley, the industry had declined. With the approval of the Corporation, therefore, Hotham was permitted to make bricks in a corner of Westwood – an operation which, according to local folk talk, was somewhat bedevilled by the disconcerting appearance of a ghost which caused temporary withdrawal of labour at the brick kiln. William Thornton, the famous York joiner, who had worked at Castle Howard and Beningbrough Hall and was currently engaged on work at the Minster, appears to have been largely responsible for the carving, panelling and for many interior fittings to Hotham's house: by May 1720, the year before he died, his account to Hotham amounted to no less than £1,116. By any standards, Sir Charles Hotham's Eastgate house in its extensive grounds must have been a town house of refinement and character but Hotham did not live long enough to enjoy it for he died in 1723. His heir and successor, the diplomat Sir Charles, the fifth Baronet, saw far less of Beverley than his father.

Ultimately, in 1766, the house and a substantial portion of the property passed into the hands of Thomas Wrightson, the builder of Ann Routh's Hospital in Keldgate. Wrightson combined building activities with those of a dealer and small-town financier, and it was probably his awareness of the possibilities of the Hotham town estate for building development which prompted him to demolish the house. About 1780 Wrightson built nos. 26 and 28 Eastgate, and other houses, unknown to their present owners, no doubt have benefited from the Wrightson pillage. An authentic token of the former Hotham house is a substantial piece of fine oak cornice – probably the work of William Thornton – which today adorns the entrance to Beverley's Art Gallery: centrally positioned thereon is the monogram of Sir Charles Hotham. In the context of Beverley's topographical history Wrightson's activities mark the initial stage of increasing misuse of the area to the north-east of the Minster: by the middle of the 19th century light industry was established there and later spread to pollute the Minster precincts and overrun the site of the neighbouring Dominican Friary.

As with the Hotham house in Eastgate, the Hall in Lairgate represents in part a similar development of an urban estate by Sir James Pennyman, one of the Borough's Members of Parliament. Pennyman did useful work for Beverley at Westminster while sitting for Scarborough and in 1774 he became Member for Beverley, where he had close family connections. After the death of his uncle Thomas in 1759 it is possible to detect from extant records more than a hint of Pennyman estate development in the neighbourhood of the Hall, including his obtaining a 21-year lease of the nearby St Giles Croft fields from the Corporation and land in the vicinity of Keldgate Bar. This coincides with the drastic remodelling of, and additions to, Pennyman House. The last private occupier of the Hall, Admiral Charles Francis Walker, died in 1925, and eventually the Hall was taken over and became the town's administrative headquarters:* in the decade before the Second World War the park land around the Hall was developed for housing.

Pennyman House is a building of high quality and Sir James, who had something of a reputation as a spendthrift, clearly spared no pains over decoration and interior embellishment. The visitor enters a hall from which rises a spacious cantilevered staircase beneath a domed light. Off the hall is a music or drawing room with bowed southern end. This Chinese Room, so called because of its high-quality hand-painted 'Chinese' wallpaper, has an exquisite plasterwork ceiling. The artist-craftsman has yet to be identified but stylistically this 'Adamesque' ceiling bears a close resemblance to the known work of the ingenious Mr Joseph Rose who died in 1799.

But Beverley's heritage of Georgian buildings comprises more than family houses. The quiet, architecturally unpretentious Charles Warton's Hospital in Minstermoorgate, for instance, is one early 18th-century building (1712) which with almshouses, like Tymperon's Almshouses in Walkergate, reflects pious local benevolence, for by 1800 Beverley had become well endowed with charities of one type or another. For some 150 years, until it closed in 1890, Beverley's Blue Coat School, which was founded in 1709, was housed in the delightful early Georgian red-brick house which meekly faces the Minster across the lawn of the church's new 'Georgian' vicarage. In Keldgate, not far away, and gable-ended to the street, is Ann Routh's Hospital which was built in 1749 by Thomas Wrightson: it was designed by James Moyser and cost £387. In 1810 the

---

* Since sold and now the offices of local firms.

Lairgate Hall.

Corporation, as trustees, contracted with the local builder-architect John Prattman for an extension to the hospital. Prattman's addition, although physically separated from the main block, sympathetically continues the stylistic treatment of the 1749 gable and thus helps to give an artistic unity to the whole.

Just as a village today has its hall, so a social requirement of the 18th-century town and community was a public meeting place for concerts, balls and similar purposes. Beverley's first Assembly Rooms were in North Bar Street near to the junction with Lairgate. There, for example, the Corporation would accord hospitality to His Majesty's judges as they travelled from Hull on their way to the assizes at York: such hospitality usually took the form of what was ingenuously known as 'a cold treat'. These Assembly Rooms served a useful purpose in other ways and John Courtney of Beverley could record approvingly, and with due priorities, that there was 'a very splendid show of ladies and gentlemen and a very agreeable ball' there on Thursday, 29 March 1759. Between 1761 and 1763, to the design of John Carr of York, William Middleton built new Assembly Rooms in Norwood on ground purchased from Charles Witty. The scheme was financed by the issue of £25 shares and the list of subscribers – Warton and Pennyman, Hildyard and Gee among them – is an *omnium gatherum* in itself of town and Riding respectability. The site cost £210, John Carr was

The Assembly Rooms.

paid 10 guineas for his plans and Middleton £790 for executing them. Considering that furnishings amounted to c.£170 and 'lustres' were almost £150, it is probably understandable that the cost of the Assembly Rooms project was underestimated and that a mortgage had to be raised to meet the deficiency. The ultimate fate of Beverley's 18th-century Assembly Rooms, which in 1900 re-echoed the oratory of the young Winston Churchill, was a sad one: reconstructed, the building became the Regal Cinema.*

Beverley's other Georgian buildings include houses like mid 18th-century Norwood House, once the home of the Beverley family (Alderman William Beverley, who died in 1843, was the son of Robert Beverley, a first cousin of George Washington, and the father of the pamphleteer, Robert Mackenzie Beverley). The fine terrace on the west side of North Bar Within and the White Horse in Hengate (basically 17th-century) also cannot fail to be noticed. The 19th-century Sessions House was completed in 1824, being built by Appleton Bennison of Hull to the design of the architect Charles Watson of York. Reticently it withdraws behind wide-spreading trees, but publicises its function† by means of a figure of yet

---

* In 1839-40 a public hall designed by Hull architect H. F. Lockwood was added to the Georgian Assembly Rooms. It was incorporated into the cinema conversion of 1935, but, after long disuse, it was eventually demolished to make way for flats and shops.
† Now sold and converted to commercial use.

Beverley Arms.

Beverley Arms: the old kitchen.

Norwood House.

Norwood House, the garden front.

another unblindfolded Justice and, moreover, gives additional character to Beverley's splendid New Walk. The old 'Blew Bell Inne' opposite St Mary's is worthy of special remark: it was extensively rebuilt by Middleton and his son John in 1794, became the Beverley Arms Hotel and in due course the 'Percy Standard' of Anthony Trollope's novel, *Ralph the Heir*. Only a few years later, Henry Ellison was building St Mary's Manor and getting into difficulties with the churchwardens of St Mary's and the Corporation alike over completion of his plans. Later restoration sometimes – as in the case of Sir Michael Warton's 17th-century Bar House, the 20th-century home of F. W. Elwell, RA – has far too effectively masked intrinsic character. But he who chooses to walk Beverley's oldest streets does not need to be unusually discerning or knowledgeable in matters of architecture to see in many smaller buildings, and in the upper part of façades long ago castrated by later shopfronts, examples of the work of 18th-century builders. No doubt armed with their copies of Langley's *Builders Jewel* and Halfpenny's *Practical Architecture*, they helped to give central Beverley the distinctively Georgian character which it has today.

After 1750 the gradual move towards an improved and more civilised urban environment becomes more marked. Inevitably the old watercourses in the streets had long been sewers in the more modern sense of the term. Although a long-term process, opportunity was taken to 'arch over' the main ones. This might be done on individual initiative, as in the case of Marmaduke Constable in 1757 and Richard Meadley in 1762, who sought and were given permission to build over open drains near the Minster. Beverley was understandably healthier than the faster-growing towns but a squeamish public health consciousness was gradually becoming evident. In 1826, William Beverley of Norwood House and Henry Ellison of St Mary's Manor agreed, in concert with the Corporation, to pay one third each of the cost to cover over the sewer in Pighill Lane so that an end could be put to 'the stench and danger arising from its open state'. In 1832 Alderman Dr Thomas Hull, energetically but unsuccessfully, proposed that the offensive Bar Dyke, outside the North Bar, be filled in and the road widened – an improvement which did not materialise until 1867. All of this is a reminder that the history of the 18th-century town is not to be construed wholly in terms of chandelier-lit assemblies and Georgian building façades.

Beverley's more important streets were paved with cobbles, largely supplied by the Constable family of Burton Constable, who, by virtue of their Holderness foreshore rights, were large-scale suppliers over a wide area. Cuthbert Constable, for example, in 1735 provided the Corporation with 204 tons at a cost of £5. 2s. 0d. Cobbles had long been used but apparently it was by no means unknown for Beverlonians furtively to 'gather furthe' and privily spirit away for private use cobbles which had been provided for the streets: this is clear from a town order of 1601 which sought to make sinners disgorge their ill-gotten gains under a threat of a ten shillings fine. Until the days of macadamising, the cobbled street was characteristic of the town and could be surprisingly rowdy beneath horses' hooves and ironshod wheels. As part of general improvement, the many public wells in the town, which excited the interest of Celia Fiennes in 1697 (she thought they were 'in imitation of Holland'), were gradually replaced by pumps. Much improvement was effected by commissioners under a town improvement Act of 1808. The town, for example, was first lit by gas in 1824, and, taking advantage of the facilities offered by the new gas works, a balloonist named Brown made what was described as a 'splendid ascent' in 1826 – an excursion which ended somewhat disastrously near Thorne.

As an example of a deliberately planned betterment scheme, owing something initially to local resident initiative, the laying out of New Walk, outside the North Bar, is worthy of notice. A walk or promenade, with trees and seats, was not only a desirable environmental improvement for families in the immediate neighbourhood but an additional amenity for the town as a whole. It is significant that York's 'New Walk' beside the Ouse was being laid out c.1732 at a time when the city's Assembly Rooms were being built. At Beverley similar development, too, is broadly coincidental. An early reference to Beverley's New Walk project is in 1779 when the Corporation agreed to subscribe £20 towards paving and making the causeway as far as the turnpike house 'as soon as the gentlemen and ladies have subscribed £30 towards the same'. (The turnpike house was situated immediately to the north of where the Sessions House is today.) New Walk was fenced in, 'formed into a regular walk and plantation', and provided with seats for the benefit of the public. The 1808 Improvement Act established commissioners with powers to levy rates for the lighting, watching and regulating of the streets, a section of the Act taking special cognisance of New Walk: any act of vandalism therein affecting trees, seats, etc. could mean a fine of £5 for the offender – no mean sum in 1808.

But a price had to be paid for town improvement. The 18th-century Corporation was not preservationist in the modern sense of the term and in 1790, for instance, for a reason not now apparent, it ordered Newbegin Bar to be taken down: in 1808 the ruined remains of Keldgate Bar were directed to be sold off. This Bar had long been in a poor state but under the terms of a 99-year lease granted to Edward Todd the Corporation had managed to derive a princely rent of 6d. per annum for the building since 1711. In 1811 it was decided to demolish property in the occupation of John Marples across the north end of Wednesday Market, obviously to facilitate access into Butcher Row. A weekly market in Wednesday Market Place had almost ended by c.1730* and, as the minor internal by-pass of Lord Roberts Road was not opened till 1909, traffic was virtually compelled to take the Butcher Row-Toll Gavel line through the town. Also

---

* A Wednesday market has been revived and a larger market held there on a Saturday.

in 1811, part of the Valiant Soldier at the junction of Norwood and Walkergate – historically, the first instalment of mutilation of that hostelry in the name of improvement – was demolished to widen the access into Norwood from Hengate and Walkergate. It is possible that this bore some relationship to the question of approach to the Assembly Rooms. Traffic problems and one-way systems in Beverley are not solely a feature of the age of the motor vehicle: when the Assembly Rooms were opened in 1763 hackney coachmen with passengers were directed to come and go by Hengate but otherwise to use Walkergate.

In an age when, by modern standards, road communications were less than adequate, the Corporation was understandably concerned to ensure the maintenance of the Beck which linked the town's port at Beckside with the navigable River Hull. The necessity of keeping the channel deep enough for the river craft which used it is apparent when it is realised that nearly all the watercourses along which Beverley had developed ran into the Beck. Because of this, and the fact that river tidal action was sluggish, there was a speedy build-up of detritus and organic matter and therefore a rapid growth of weed. Between 1700 and 1725 technical approaches to the problem of 'skowringe' the Beck were considered but the whole question was basically financial. Accordingly in 1727 an Act of Parliament, amended by a second in 1745, was obtained to authorise the collection of dues on all goods shipped or landed within the town's liberties. Financially this legislation was worthwhile, for more money was raised for the maintenance, not only of the Beck, but of the streets and roads leading down to the Beck and the landing places on the river within the town's liberties, like Grovehill and Hull Bridge.

In 1798 the Beverley and Barmston Drainage Scheme, which was begun under an Act of Parliament of that year, resulted in the cutting of the drain at a significantly lower level than the River Hull. It was obviously considered that such regional drainage improvement would lower the level of the river and that therefore the making of a lock was necessary to preserve the level of water in the Beck. The lock was completed in 1802, thereby making the Beck a more stagnant waterway and creating a public health problem of some consequence.

Until 1729, when it was taken down, the High Bridge, as it was called, crossed the Beck at a point some 80 yards from the western end of the navigation where the Low Bridge (earlier known as Parson's Bridge) carried the road past the old St Nicholas churchyard. Into Beverley's Beck came keel and river craft like *Hull Trader, Hopewell, Endeavour* and *Satisfaction,* bringing coal, turves, bricks, tiles, building stone, iron, salt, flour, wine and a wide range of miscellaneous goods from places like Hull, Thorne and Knottingley. Outward from Beverley went leather, butter and malt, and occasionally unspecifiable cargoes like the '½ tun of old Junck' on which a toll of 2d. was paid in 1745. In economic terms, Beverley's Beck was very much Beverley's lifeline before the age of the railway.

As a regional capital, market town and social centre, Beverley was increasingly aware of the need for improved communications. In 1744, after three years of diplomatic manoeuvring, Hull and Beverley secured an Act for turnpiking the road from Hull to Beverley. This meant that designated commissioners, as trustees, were charged with repair of the highway and were empowered to invite investment in the scheme and to charge toll at specific points for the public use of the road: such tolls were for the repair of the road and for the payment of interest on moneys invested. It is a reflection of the mutual suspicion which prevailed between Hull and Beverley Corporations that the Act had to specify that the trustees should determine by lot where repair should begin. A mile of road was then to be repaired, to be followed by a mile from the other terminal point. The first meeting of the trustees was to be at the White Horse in Beverley and the second at the King's Head in Hull, and thereafter as the trustees themselves should decide. Thus, from 1744, the Hull-Beverley road was a turnpike and all users, apart from pedestrians, paid appropriate toll until the road was disturnpiked in 1871. Under the 1744 Act a man on horseback going to Hull paid 6d. toll and a coach with two horses 9d.: these payments also covered the return journey provided it was made before midnight. In the middle years of the century Beverley Corporation took an active part in the implementation of local turnpiking schemes.

★ ★ ★

The church of St Nicholas, near the Beck, was ruined during the Civil War. Abortive attempts were made in 1646 and again in 1648 to bring about a union of the parish with the Minster, but in 1667, under permissive legislation of 1665, Archbishop Richard Sterne decreed the union of the two benefices of St Mary's and St Nicholas. Until the new St Nicholas church was consecrated in 1880, St Mary's was the only church serving the two parishes. The St Nicholas site, with and without archiepiscopal permission, was plundered of building stone for the repair of the Minster and St Mary's, and, although Alderman Marmaduke Nelson, writing c.1710, could claim remembrance of St Nicholas tower standing, it is clear that before the end of the 17th century the last vestiges of the medieval church had disappeared.

That the Minster needed more than mere repair was palpably evident by the time Nelson was making his historical notes. Some serious but unspecified repairs were made to the fabric in 1613 and a cart and four oxen were bought to bring stones from the site of Watton Priory. After 1660 a considerable 'cleaning up operation', which included new pews and pulpit, was carried out. It is possible that an earthquake shock on 28 December 1703, worsened the condition of the Minster fabric insofar as the gable of the great north transept was concerned. A brief was secured, but financial difficulties ensued, and in 1717 Sir Michael Warton, with Nicholas Hawksmoor, issued an appeal for funds, a plea which was given reinforced urgency six months later, following a survey of the Minster by a local mason, Thackeray, when it was clear disaster was very near. The restoration projects which followed included obtaining licence from the Crown in 1718 to take stone from the site of St Mary's Abbey at York for a period of three years, and the spectacular rocking back into position of the north transept gable in a massive timber cradle, which obviated the necessity of a rebuild. The great frame, operated by screws, was in position for some 12 months from September 1719. William Thornton of York is usually credited with this daring repair project. Writing before 1736, Francis Drake, the author of *Eboracum*, thought that Thornton's 'reparation of Beverley Minster ought to give him a lasting memorial', an opinion that would seem to discount the possibility of the reticent Hawksmoor having any concern with the project which, on the evidence, is highly unlikely. Although not the only modern example, it is interesting to note that in 1958, when the south wall of the nave of the Romanesque church of Saint-Martin d'Aime, near Moûtiers in Savoy, was restored in exactly the same way, it was acknowledged that the origin of the technique was to be found in this early-18th-century restoration of the great north transept gable of Beverley Minster.

With the repair of the north transept gable, other essential work was carried out. Externally, the silhouette of the church was radically altered in 1721 by the addition of a cupola; this replaced an octagonal lantern on the central stub tower which was itself reconstructed. The reason for such an inelegant, if fashionable, onion-like embellishment is unknown, although it may be remarked that a small one pouted forth from the central tower of York Minster between 1666 and 1728. In 1756 John Carr was commissioned to prepare plans for 'a new steeple' and it is possible that the intention even then was to remove the excrescence: as it happened, this architectural tumour was not excised until 1824.

The parlous state of the fabric aroused county sympathy and resulted in substantial gifts being forthcoming (the king's contribution alone being £100, less 7s. 6d. tax). The energy with which the restoration work was pushed forward owed much to Sir Michael Warton, Nicholas Hawksmoor, and in particular to John Moyser. The last named was sufficiently alert to the potential dangers inherent in a situation in which an impoverished town Corporation was administering specially raised funds, and he found it necessary in 1720 to make allegations of the Corporation's misappropriation of Minster moneys. The storm blew over but not before the mayor and some of his brethren had visited Bishopthorpe, following the preparation of accounts for examination by the archbishop.

By his will, Sir Michael Warton, who died in 1725, bequeathed £4,000 as a permanent fund for the repair of the fabric and in 1747 moneys from the Minster 'New Fund' were invested in land in Lincolnshire. As a result of this windfall and of other gifts, 'beautification' of the church in the Georgian manner confidently went ahead – a baroque font cover from the Thorntons' workshop at York, galleries, a magnificently overpowering reredos and baldachino, a pulpitum, and a re-flooring of nave and chancel (the latter with Italian marble shipped from Leghorn by Wilberforce of Hull), were the main features of the work. Carvers like John Pale and John Healey were busy but, in the middle of it all, Nicholas Hawksmoor was not forgotten – in 1735, the year before he died, he received a gift of knives and forks.

The work was largely completed before 1760 and the building of an organ for which Thomas Haxby of York submitted a design in 1762 was being considered. A specially solicited Act of Parliament in 1766 authorising some reorganisation of Warton's benefaction allowed more money to be available for the minister and curates and also for building an organ and providing an organist. Matthias Hawdon was appointed organist, and the fact that funds were not lacking is illustrated by John Snetzler's account for the organ he built in 1768-69 which cost over £700 – a sum exclusive of transport costs. The organ was 'opened' (as the contemporary expression had it) in September 1769 with a three-day music festival devoted to three major works of Handel – *Messiah, Judas Maccabeus,* and *Samson* – and concluding with his *Coronation Anthem.* At this festival, the first to be held in the north of England, the star performer with the specially surpliced singers was the brilliant violinist, Felice de Giardini.

The Minster's state of comparative financial well-being continued and a second Act of Parliament obtained in 1806 allowed additional augmentation of clergy and organist's stipends and the appointment of another assistant curate. But inevitably, there had been deterioration in the fabric, and, following an inspection by John Cliffe in 1812, William Shout, the master mason at York Minster, carried out a survey which showed that much had to be done. The next year, Shout's former apprentice, William Comins, began his long association with the Minster as superintendent mason which lasted until his death in 1836 and marks a period of Gothic revival and much sympathetic restoration, contrasting strikingly with the work of a century earlier. By 1835 the galleries, the classical baldachino over the altar and other 18th-century additions had been removed and the choir restored under plans prepared by Thomas Rickman and Henry Atkinson, with William Fowler of Winterton as supervising architect. The Georgian pulpitum lasted until 1875, by which time plans were in hand to replace it.

As far as the fabric of St Mary's was concerned, no major rebuilding or restoration project appears to have been necessary within the period with which we are here directly concerned. The Tudor builders, after the disaster of 1520, had apparently done a good job, and in 1585 a grant by the Crown of properties in Beverley, which by the early years of the 19th century were producing approximately £800 per annum, provided a useful continuing income for fabric maintenance and general church purposes. Like the Minster, St Mary's from the 17th century was subjected to characteristic interior furnishings, the first gallery or loft being built on the north of the nave as early as 1616, the pews therein being let out at rent. In 1756 this gallery was rebuilt but in the intervening period additional galleried seating arrangements provided an 18th-century picture of a gallery and nave congregation facing each other and centring on a three-decker pulpit of 1734 – all of which symbolises the penchant of the 18th-century churchgoer for goodly slabs of pulpit oratory. It no doubt also explains why, in 1741, the more penurious churchwardens of nearby Scorborough were able to acquire the old pulpit at the give-away price of 19s. After 1791 with the acquisition of an organ, towards which the Corporation subscribed 40 guineas, the view eastwards was further restricted with the positioning of the instrument under the crossing immediately to the south of the Corporation's canopied pews.

The fact that after 1581 the Corporation were accorded the right of appointing and dismissing the Minster clergy meant that until the Municipal Corporations Act of 1835 the ministers there tended to reflect more accurately the Corporation's own Puritan-Low Church views. Thomas Whincop (1583-99) was a Puritan-minded scholar whose supervisory duties in matters theological over some of the local clergy may well have been daunting: at least in 1594 the parsons of Routh, Leven and Long Riston were summoned before the archbishop's court at York to explain why they had not repaired to Mr. Whincop with their 'exercises' as ordered. Whincop became Master of the Charterhouse at Hull and his 'Shakespearian' memorial bust can be seen high up on the south aisle wall of the chancel of Holy Trinity, the smallness of the lettering of the accompanying substantial inscription confounding the non-Latinist and short-sighted alike. Whincop was followed by William Crashaw (1599-1605), vigorous anti-Papal preacher, outstanding Biblical scholar and bibliophile and the father of the poet Richard Crashaw, who entered the Roman Catholic church and died a beneficed priest of Our Lady of Loreto in Rome.

At the other end of the timescale covered by this present chapter, Joseph Coltman may be noted, not only because, as a weighty cleric of some 37 stones, his portly form has been publicised widely in silhouette complete with dandy, but because of his educational and charitable work in Beverley. A man of wide scholarship and sturdy principle, he was granted the freedom of the Borough in 1810 for the care he gave to the Blue Coat school in Highgate. But not least of the rigours he set himself and others was his habit of reading Latin and Greek authors with the boys at the Grammar School before breakfast. As the writer of his obituary notice charmingly and naively put it in 1837, 'Of a truth it may be said a great man has fallen in Beverley.' Not all the Minster clergy attained the high personal standards of a Whincop, Crashaw or Coltman and when discipline was necessary the Corporation could be Puritanically stern, as the Revd Thomas Lewthwaite found in 1744 when he and his assistant, James

Graves, were in trouble for not visiting the sick. Additionally, the appropriately named Graves was charged with refusing burial and leaving the deceased poor overnight in the Minster until the burial fee was raised. This minor scandal was not held permanently against Graves for he succeeded to the Minster curacy on Lewthwaite's death in 1779.

The Corporation had no prerogative of choice in respect of the St Mary's clergy for the advowson was in the hands of the Crown. But, when occasion required, influence could be brought to bear and in 1766 the Corporation, with an indelicacy which was not unusual in the 18th century, was busy soliciting the Lord Chancellor on behalf of one party some time before the incumbent, the Revd Samuel Johnston, died. The Corporation's efforts on this occasion were unsuccessful and the Revd Francis Drake, the eldest son of the author of *Eboracum*, was inducted. But in 1791 the Corporation fared better and, when in turn Drake was nearing the end of his life, they petitioned the Lord Chancellor, the Archbishop and the Duke of Leeds on behalf of the curate, the Revd Robert Rigby. Rigby was a popular cleric and, soon after his appointment as vicar, received the Borough freedom as testimony of 'approbation of his conduct as a clergyman'. In 1802 he was invited to join the aldermanic circle – the first clergyman in modern times to be a member of the town's chamber.

The only parson of St Mary's who achieved any degree of notoriety was John Brereton whom the Corporation obliged to resign the benefice in 1689. Brereton became vicar in 1672; and in 1684, mingling the spiritual and the material, he made the Corporation a series of gifts which included a large Book of Common Prayer and a silver tankard, for which acts of clerical kindliness he was 'esteemed by the Corporation as one of their great benefactors'. But the esteem in which Brereton was held melted rapidly when in 1689 it was discovered that he had appropriated the proceeds of several church collections as well as a large sum of money collected in the town for the relief of Huguenots following the revocation of the Edict of Nantes.

Congregationalism in Beverley has a long and impressive history and in a town by no means lacking in Puritan sympathies it is understandable why Nonconformity struck deep roots: 1689, when the Toleration Act was passed, is also the year of the first indications of an independent Meeting House in the town. This was on a site at the junction of Well Lane and Cross Street.* William Foster was the preacher at the conventicle here which, judging by memoranda in the Minster parish register of the time, clearly aroused the ire of the Revd William Davies, one of the Minster curates. The Well Lane congregation grew and in 1700 land was bought in Lairgate and a new Meeting House built which, unfortunately, was destroyed by a great storm in 1715. The speedy rebuilding of the church at

---

* VCH p.250 calls them Presbyterians rather than Congregationalists and also suggests the move to Lairgate was made by 1694.

No. 7 Hengate, 1708-9

Nos. 90-92 Walkergate, built c.1755.

Sessions House.

a time when finances were straitened is testimony to the existence of a virile congregation, the members of which, it is known, did not wholly derive from Beverley. In 1800, during the ministry of the Revd Peter Feist (1790-1807), this church was replaced by yet a third – an attractively simple building and architecturally very characteristic of the period.

At the age of 35 John Wesley began his great personal evangelising crusade and it is computed that in a 52 years' mission he must have travelled a quarter of a million miles and preached 40,000 sermons: Beverley saw him on at least 17 separate occasions. On his first visit (July 1759) he preached in 'Mr Hilton's yard near the great street' at 8 o'clock in the morning and remarked on his quiet and civil reception in the town. By his third visit (1764) a congregation had developed and the Cock Pit in Wood Lane became the Beverley Preaching House. Both Wesley and George Whitefield received considerable support from Sir Charles Hotham, the sixth Baronet. Whitefield, for example, had preached in Sir Charles Hotham's yard in Eastgate in 1760 – a sermon which John Courtney pithily and uncharitably dismissed as 'Poor Discourse!' In 1766 (17 July) Wesley called on Sir Charles and 'spent a comfortable hour' there prior to going to Hull. He recorded a visit to the Minster – 'a parish church which has scarce its fellow in England' and was 'kept more nicely clean' than any cathedral he had seen. Nevertheless he did not dwell on the beauties of Gothic architecture for he was immediately minded to speculate where the Minster would be 'when the earth is burned up and the elements melt with the fervent heat'.

The Beverley Methodist congregation increased in numbers and strength, the Wood Lane Preaching House was enlarged and in 1804 preparations were made to remove to a new site in Walkergate, where a chapel was opened in 1805. The problems and difficulties over organisation and discipline which beset Methodism after Wesley's death are illustrated in Beverley by the building of the Primitive Methodists' chapel in Wednesday Market in 1825. In the same year a splinter group, calling themselves Church Methodists, primarily concerned over matters of Methodist separation from the Church of England, built a Church Methodist chapel at the junction of Landress Lane and Lairgate under the active leadership of Mark Robinson and Anthony Atkinson. This chapel was ultimately demolished after lengthy sectarian wrangling and the materials used for the building of St John's chapel* in Lairgate, which was opened in 1840. The former St John's chapel is now the town's Memorial Hall, the present Congregational schoolroom being built in 1879 on the site of the former Church Methodist chapel.

Two Baptist congregations representing slight differences in doctrine and polity had their churches in the town – the one meeting in a room in Toll Gavel early in the 19th century and the second in a small chapel built

*An Anglican chapel, a subsidiary of the Minster.

in 1808 in Swaby's Yard, off Walkergate. In 1834 a new chapel was sited in Well Lane only to be sacrificed for improvement when Lord Roberts Road was laid out in 1909: its successor, dating from 1910,* on the corner site in Lord Roberts Road, has now been closed. Another Nonconformist group, the Society of Friends, small in numbers at the beginning of the last century, had its meeting house in Wood Lane.

★   ★   ★

Until 1816, when it moved into Keldgate, the town's grammar school was in the south-west corner of the Minster churchyard in a picturesque early 17th-century building which consisted of schoolroom and master's house. In 1773 the Revd George Croft, the master of the school, made private proposals to the Corporation for the building of a house in Keldgate which he then apparently occupied: the rent of this house – now the Old School House – was added by the Corporation to the emoluments of the mastership soon after Croft resigned in 1780. In 1816 John Cliff built the new school in Keldgate near the master's house. In one sense this expulsion of the school from the Minster churchyard can be regarded not only as part and parcel of the contemporary Minster restoration scheme but as an insurance against damage in the future. As early as 1784 the Corporation had found it necessary to inform Croft's successor, the Revd John Jackson, that his application for certain repairs to glass windows at the school was unreasonable and there is no reason to think that the Minster's windows were inevitably immune from damage. From the middle of the 17th century the school was in a flourishing condition – Marmaduke Nelson, writing c.1700, remembered it in his day as a school of 140-150 boys and Celia Fiennes recorded it in 1697 as having a reputation as 'the best in England for learning and care'. The school's importance and prosperity owed greatly to a succession of masters like Joseph Lambert, John Clarke and George Croft, and a close connection with St John's College, Cambridge which, with Christ's College, Cambridge, was a foundation indissolubly linked with the name of Bishop John Fisher, the school's distinguished alumnus.

But the grammar school and the Blue Coat school were not the only educational institutions in the town. At least from the second half of the 17th century schoolmasters like John Norris and his successor Thomas Marshall were teaching children in St Mary's church — presumably the 'Priest's Room' there was the schoolroom. By 1743 Thomas Mease, the curate of the Minster, could testify to the existence of several 'petty' schools in his parish. Additional educational provision was made possible by the bequest of the Revd James Graves, who died in 1807. Under this benefaction boys' and girls' schools were set up in the town in 1810 and four years later became established in the old theatre in Register Square. In

---

*Currently used by East Riding of Yorkshire Archives Services.

1815 a school under the auspices of the National Society for promoting the Education of the Poor was begun in Minstermoorgate, supported by the Corporation and by private subscription: the National school flourished considerably following the substantial charitable bequest of Christopher Eden, a Beverley corn merchant who died in 1823.

An increasing number of private schools can be noticed after 1800 – David Hick's Commercial Academy, Mrs. Hall's school in St John Street, Miss Sandwith's in North Bar Street, and Mrs Amery's in Flemingate among others: there was a dancing school in Toll Gavel and the Revd William Hildyard had his ordination school in Walkergate. These, and many others, came into being to meet the varying and increasing needs in an age of rapid change: it is unfortunate that, for the most part, the fact that they existed is virtually all that is known about them.

★   ★   ★

Beverley had sent representative burgesses to various Parliaments in medieval times but Elizabeth's charter of 1573 stabilised the position. Initially regarded as an expense for the Borough and a chore for the Member, service at Westminster in due course came to be seen as one conferring privilege and offering socially profitable opportunities. Understandably, a burgess who was prepared to serve at personal charge was welcomed and after 1660 it was consistently the practice for the Borough to make an agreement with its Members on these lines to obviate the risk of executors making retrospective statutory expenses claims.

Until the early 18th century, choice of the two Members was more a matter of selection than election but the entry of a third party into the arena – as was first the case in 1722 – forced an election which naturally stimulated the wholesale wooing of the burgess vote by various forms of inducement: and, of course, for the most part and for obvious reasons, the burgesses were only too willing to be both wooed and seduced.

Although the Borough was in no one's pocket, the Warton and Hotham interests were well to the fore in the late 17th and early 18th centuries. The direct and active influence of the Hothams lasted until the death of Sir Charles, the fifth Baronet, in 1734, but the Warton-Pelham concern with the Borough continued for another half century. But burgess electoral allegiance could speedily change with an early canvass of freemen, the flashing of a newcomer's guineas and, opportunities provided of sampling new election fleshpots. The unholy reputation which the town acquired by the middle years of the 19th century was by no means unique, but it stemmed from a sophistication born of long experience in the management of contested elections. It is some measure of the Borough's national notoriety in matters of elections that the one in 1727 led directly to the 1729 statute against bribery, and the evidence dredged up by the Royal Commission on Beverley in 1869 provided much ammunition which helped to get the Ballot Bill through Parliament in 1872.

Like any other borough, Beverley found its Members of Parliament quite useful apart from their legislative and watchdog functions at Westminster. It paid a Member to keep his seat warm and give the aldermen a treat at Christmas or New Year. When subscriptions were required for a new Market Cross, the relief of the poor, racing on the Westwood or the salary of the master of the grammar school, he could often be a very present help in trouble: the popularity of a Member was in fact largely to be measured by the capacity of his pocket and his willingness to put his hand in it.

★   ★   ★

As part of the restored Stuarts' policy of ensuring that only the well-affected held civic office and, therefore, would return right-thinking men to Westminster, Beverley, like other boroughs, was purged of dissidents under the Corporations Act of 1661 and 6 of the 13 governors lost office. Like other corporations, too, the Borough was pressurised by Writ of *Quo Warranto* in the last years of Charles' reign and surrendered its charter of 1663. The acquisition of a new one in 1685, which became the town's governing charter until municipal reform, involved the Corporation in expenses amounting to some £438 for the stay of three of the governors in London to transact the necessary legal business: a financially embarrassed Corporation could only reward these civic plenipotentiaries with 40s. each to buy a ring commemorative both of the occasion and their personal assiduity. This charter changed the name of governor to alderman and nominated the permanent body of 13 aldermen as well as the 13 capital burgesses who were annually elected by the burgesses at large from a list of 26 burgess 'lites' chosen by the aldermen.

This system of civic rule continued unchanged until the Municipal Corporations Act became effective on 1 January, 1836. Until the Age of Reform, record of local criticism of the system is virtually nil. The aldermen had the right of inviting any burgess to fill an aldermanic vacancy and a fine of £50 could follow for refusal to serve, a right which in time of civic penury could be prostituted to unworthy ends if it was known that a burgess did not wish to serve. This was clearly the thinking which prompted William Sperrin's colourful comments in 1751 when he suggested that the mayor and aldermen were rogues and pickpockets for electing the reluctant William Strickland as alderman who, refusing to serve, was mulched of £50.

In 1833, on the setting up of the Royal Commission to inquire into corporations, the exquisitely-named commissioners Fortunatus Dwarris and Samson Augustus Rumbald held a two-day inquiry in the Guildhall. The evidence offered was not so damning as in, say, the case of Hull but it tended to bear out locally expressed opinion that civic rule in Beverley was feeble, careless and extravagant. In particular, by the 1830s, there was growing resentment that capital burgesses were, in effect, of aldermanic choice. The fact is that, in the 18th century and especially so after 1750, the socio-economic class of aldermen changed markedly as the town became more residential in character. In the 25-year period 1651-75, 21 of Beverley's mayors were tradesmen or shopkeepers and 4 only could be classed as gentry or professional: between 1801 and 1825 there was only 1 tradesman mayor. As Thomas Shepherd, the town clerk, conceded at the inquiry of 1833, it was not by then the practice to select as aldermen burgesses who were engaged in trade: socially, the cleavage between alderman and burgesses at large could not be more complete.

Dwarris and Rumbald noted that Beverley's population in 1831 was 7,432 and that the town had 'a flourishing appearance'. They qualified their comment by remarking that the town's prosperity was 'said to be on the increase but not to any great extent'. How far such an impression was justified has to be considered in the context of the history of the last century and a half which is the theme of the chapter which follows.

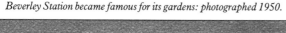

Beverley Station became famous for its gardens: photographed 1950.

6 THE VICTORIAN AGE AND AFTER

It is doubtful if Beverley's population topped its mid-Tudor level of c.5,000 before 1750. Thereafter a rise becomes apparent and between 1801 (the year of the first official census) and 1871 the number of inhabitants almost doubled from 5,401 to 10,218. This of course reflected national trends, but certainly local developments were not without their own significance: the most important were improvement of local communications and the growth of nearby Hull.

Radial road improvements, and even more so, the coming of the railway in 1846 had three definable results. Firstly, light industry was encouraged, a change which particularly affected the southern and eastern parts of the town. Secondly, as travel facilities improved, Beverley became more of a dormitory for Hull. Finally, the economic status which as a market town Beverley enjoyed within its region was gradually eroded to Hull's benefit.

East Yorkshire's first railway was the Hull and Selby which was opened in 1840. It was inevitable that railway coverage of eastern Yorkshire would come in due course. On 1 July 1840, at the gargantuan cold collation which marked the celebrations of the opening of the Hull and Selby line, His Worship the Mayor of Beverley, Anthony Atkinson, was invited to respond to the last of the 21 toasts – 'The Mayor of Beverley and other strangers with us this evening'. Whether the Mayor was flushed with liquor or merely irritated by toastal linkage with 'other strangers' is not known but he was tactless enough to comment on the fact that a survey for a Hull-Beverley railway was already in progress, irritated good Hullensians present by remarking that Hull's death rate was 25 per cent higher than Beverley's, and said that when the railway was built Hull business men might prefer to live in more salubrious Beverley. Ungentlemanly hissing on this occasion apparently obliged His Worship to draw his comments to a speedy conclusion. The Hull-Beverley line envisaged (which was to link up with the Hull-Selby) was planned to commence near the Paragon Inn in Chariot Street, Hull, and – somewhat surprisingly – terminate at the south end of St John Street near Beverley Minster. An alternative proposal was to have the Beverley station in Well Lane. What its promoters failed to realise was that such a railway would be too small to be economically viable. The railway which ultimately served Beverley was the Hull to Bridlington, a project sponsored initially by the Hull and Selby Company and taken over by George Hudson, the Railway King, when his York and North Midland Company acquired the Hull and Selby in 1845.

In general, plans for a railway were welcomed by Beverley industrialists like William Crosskill, who had founded the Beverley Iron Works in 1825, and Pennock Tigar, colour manufacturer, of Grovehill. But others saw in a railway scheme the destruction of Beverley's retail trade to Hull's advantage, a diminution of town property values and a fall in valuable Beck toll income. Daniel Boyes, the Beverley Liberal party leader, for example, roundly castigated town councillor James Mowld Robinson, one of the principal objectors to the railway, for being far too concerned over Beck tolls. Boyes commented on the fact that that particular stream was neither limpid nor fragrant and, like the Emperor Vespasian, the councillor had scented only the dues and found them 'as odiferous as the Roman Emperor did the cess-pool tax'. It was publicly suggested that as an intransigent champion of local vested interests Mr Robinson was a gentleman eminently qualified for the presidency of an antiquarian society. But Robinson and his faithful phalanx of backwoodsmen were not so obscurantist as their opponents thought – they realised only too well that Beverley's intermediate position on the railway between Beverley and Hull would inevitably rebound to the economic benefit of Hull as the major port and railway terminal.

The Corporation sold the Trinities site for the proposed railway station and a 'splendid street' (Railway Street) was planned to link station with town. George Townsend Andrews, who worked closely with Hudson, was the architect for the station and before the end of June 1846 a locomotive was running to and fro along the new railway line. As one scribe put it, 'The quiet folks of Beverley are almost frightened out of their property by the shrill whistle and rumbling of truck wagons which almost every hour sound to the remotest parts of the town.' But Beverley took it all in its stride and on 6 October 1846, to celebrate the opening of the line and deigning to stop en route at Beverley, three locomotives, *Aerial*, *Antelope*, and inevitably, *Hudson*, drew a distinctly bizarre and motley ensemble of rolling stock through from Hull to Bridlington for the initial celebrations. Beverley's (now disused) rail connection with York did not come until 1865 when the Beverley-Market Weighton section was opened to join up with the York-Market Weighton line which Hudson had built in 1847. It is interesting to note that the town was also associated with two other schemes, both of which failed to come to fruition: one was a plan by Hudson to build a line from Beverley to Hornsea (with a junction at Arram) and the second a scheme authorised under the North Holderness Light Railway Act of 1898 for a link with North Frodingham. Had these materialised their survival in the post-Beeching era would have been more than dubious.

*   *   *

Thanks to a plentiful water supply and local availability of oak bark, tanning was an important industry early in the town's history and as late as 1752 a Brotherhood of Tanners, lineal descendants of the medieval tanners' gild, still existed. William Hodgson of Gainford in County Durham was in Beverley in 1812 and began the building up of the firm of Richard Hodgson and Sons which was ultimately acquired in 1920 by Messrs Barrow, Hepburn and Gale. There were other tanneries in the town in these years: one in Keldgate, which was being worked by William Simpson c.1820, came into the hand of the locally important Cussons family. Later this business was reorganised in 1939 as Melrose Tanners and maintained an independent existence until acquired by Messrs Booth and Company Limited in 1948.

For at least 200 years shipbuilding has been carried on at Grovehill on the River Hull, east of the town. In 1763 Richard Hopwood was building vessels there: the development of the industry naturally reflected the growing river and canal trade. Some sizeable vessels were built, including *Beverlac** for Pennock Tigar, which was launched in 1829, destined for the London trade. From c.1890 the phenomenal development of the Hull fishing industry and the introduction of steam trawlers correlated closely with the expansion of shipbuilding at Grovehill. This was particularly marked after the acquisition of the yard by the Hull firm of Cook, Welton and Gemmell in 1902. Between 1882 (when the firm was founded) and the outbreak of war in 1939, and despite the economic recession of the 1920s and 1930s, Messrs Cook, Welton and Gemmell could justifiably claim that theirs indeed was a firm that had launched a thousand ships – most of them by a spectacular sideways launch into the narrow River Hull. But shipbuilding was not the only industry on the river at Grovehill. Pennock Tigar of Grove House, a leading Liberal in the town, had his paint and colour factory there before 1830: after his death in 1851 the business was sold and fertilisers took the place of paints and colours. A corn miller, Josiah Crathorne, was also established at Grovehill early in Victoria's reign: the destruction by fire of Crathorne's Mill in 1907 was probably one of the most spectacular conflagrations the town had ever seen.

Industrial development also came in the vicinity of the railway station. Nearly a quarter of a century before the Bridlington line was opened, the young William Crosskill had founded his iron works in Wilbert Lane. Justifiably, Crosskill can be regarded as the father of mechanised farming in East Yorkshire. He had a national reputation as a maker of agricultural machinery, being awarded the Gold Medal of the Royal Agricultural Society for his patent clodcrusher and, at the Great Exhibition of 1851, the Council's Medal for his Norwegian harrow and other farming implements. The Crosskill business boomed during the Crimean War when the firm was engaged in the making of carts and shells, and the labour force employed there in 1854 was as high as 800. Crosskill's Old Foundry was bought up in 1864 and became the Beverley Iron and Waggon Company, with Sir Henry Edwards of Halifax as the company's chairman. Edwards became Member of Parliament for the Borough in 1857 and was to play a notoriously influential part in the electoral history of the town until Beverley was disfranchised in 1870. The Beverley Iron and Waggon Company came to an end in 1879. Additional to Crosskill's Old Foundry, the firm of Sawney had an agricultural implements works in Station Square (later taken over by

---

* Built by Henry Harrison.

Beverley Beck, probably early 20th century.

A launch.

the East Yorkshire Cart and Waggon Company), and Crosskill's two sons established themselves in Eastgate, also as manufacturers of farm implements.

In exactly the same way, other town businesses of importance were built up as a result of individual enterprise. The old established firm of Robert Stephenson and Son brewed ale behind the Golden Ball in Toll Gavel, almost cheek by jowl with the Wesleyan chapel in Walkergate. John Cherry, brick and tile maker of Hornsea, began to experiment with the making of pumps in the 1880s: success led him to transfer to premises in Beverley and to establish a business which today sends Beverley-made pumps to all parts of the world.* In 1909 Gordon Armstrong began business as a small garage proprietor and in 1913 built a motor car:† today, Armstrong's shock absorbers and suspension units are used on the majority of English as well as on many foreign cars. In 1878 the enterprising young John Watts of Hull (formerly of Brigg) acquired the Beverley carrier business of J. Backhouse and, with emphasis on meticulous timing, thereby establishing a wholesome precedent for the future, saw to it that Watt's Waggon left Beverley each day for Hull precisely at 8 am and returned from the Rampant Horse in Mytongate at 2 pm, connecting up with other carriers in and out of Hull. These were the pioneer beginnings of a transport firm which today, like others in the town, can rightly claim a fine record of public service.‡ Printing, too, had early formed an important part of the town's activities. As early as 1509 Hugo Goes, said to have been the son of an Antwerp printer, is reputed to have established a printing press 'in the Highgate' (not necessarily the Highgate of today) but after a time moved on to London. Early last century there were three printers in the town, one of them, Matthew Turner, in 1829 printing and publishing George Oliver's *History of Beverley.* The oldest of these printing businesses was probably that of John Green, who opened a shop in Hengate as a printer and bookbinder in 1793, the family taking over the Saturday Market establishment of James Ramsden in 1846.

This variegated pattern of light industry in the town has made for economic buoyancy, and official planning with its emphasis on the location of industry east of the town has helped (though not always successfully) to encourage and establish new forms of post-war economic enterprise.

★   ★   ★

The Municipal Corporations Act of 1835 meant that, with effect from 1 January, 1836, the old conciliar system of 13 permanent aldermen and 13 annually elected capital burgesses was replaced by a town council of 6

* Now closed.
† Armstrong's Eastgate factory closed in 1981.
‡ Transferred to a depot at Goole 1991.

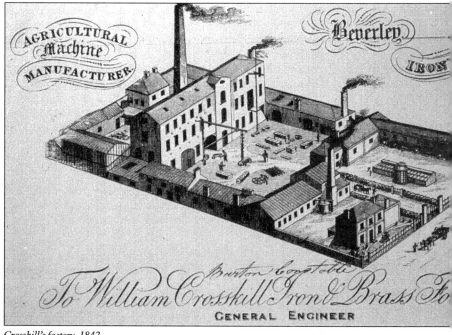

Crosskill's factory, 1842.

Armstrong's factory, Eastgate, 1968.

aldermen and 18 councillors elected by the whole body of adult male ratepayers. As elsewhere, the new broom intended to sweep clean. Councillor Pottage (who, to celebrate his newly acquired status, had his infant son baptised John Councillor Pottage) and Councillor Gillyat Sumner (in due course to acquire local notoriety as a magpie antiquary) were deputed to draw up a schedule of Corporation furnishings, plate and wines which were to be sold off as being both superfluous and frippery. With some exceptions the list was approved, one exception being a silver snuffbox, the gift in 1707 of a former chamber clerk, John Jackson. This was to be filled with snuff on Mr Mayor's directions: this was immediately done at the meeting and apparently, with what must have been singular lack of decorum, 'the members present indulged themselves in titillating the olfactory nerves'. The sale of effects only realised £88.

The new Corporation was confronted with many problems – compensation to officials deprived of office, finance, the sale of the Minster advowson (which ultimately went to the Simeon Trustees for £3,300), and, probably the most irritating of all, the matter of the pastures.

Doubts were raised in 1836 as to whether, under the Municipal Corporations Act, the new Corporation had the power to organise the election of pasture masters and to supervise the pastures. The matter aroused considerable bitterness, but ultimately supplication was made for a special Act of Parliament to clarify the position. This was obtained in 1836, the control of the common lands being vested in the resident freemen who, provided their names were on the 'Pasture Freemen's Roll', were to elect the pasture masters. The election was to be held before the mayor (or before one or more aldermen deputed by him) on 1 March each year between the hours of 9 am and 4 pm, but provision was made that, if 20 minutes elapsed during which time no vote was tendered for any candidate, the presiding officer was empowered (but not enjoined) to close the poll. Problems arose over the matter of the race course stand and in 1861 there was a riot in the town over the claim of the freemen against the Corporation in respect of the area then known as Bull Close, south of Westwood Road. In 1761 this enclosure, clearly originally a part of Westwood, had been leased for 99 years to a miller, John Maud of Sculcoates. In 1799 Robert Fishwick took over the lease and in 1861, in conformity with the terms of the original lease, his successors, John and William Wood Fishwick, surrendered the property. The Corporation took the view that Bull Close was not part of Westwood. The freemen led by John Duffill, the town's bellman, thought otherwise, stubbed up the quickwood fence and burned the mill-house. The whole business resulted in nominal fines for a few but at Quarter Session the jury threw out the bill of indictment against the ring leaders. That same night a mass of Beverlonians assembled on the site, were addressed by the redoubtable Duffill and, by acclamation, it was agreed that the stump whereon the mill had stood should in future be known as Duffill's Mound, a name which has yet to find its place on the Ordnance Survey map.

★ ★ ★

Until the parliamentary election of 1868, following which the town was disfranchised, electoral corruption assumed the character of a staple industry, national and local politics being closely linked. The 1832 Reform Act had given the vote to the £10 householders but had not excluded from the franchise the freemen who, of course, might not be householders in their own right. By the time of the Second Reform Act of 1867 it was estimated that out of a constituency of some 1,100 voters, about 800 were open to bribery and other corrupt influences, including about 300 who were without any political principles of any kind and were known locally as 'the rolling stock' because of their propensity for rolling to the party which offered the greatest inducements. Additionally, there were about 250 others who expected to be paid what were, in effect, retainer fees by their own party candidates: these only regarded payment as a bribe when it came from the other party. Voting was, of course, public and poll books were printed showing how the individual had voted. Elections were invariably marked by colourful incident.

At the by-election of 1840 the Tories were fearful that, with the Liberal tide turning against them, their poor quality candidate, Sackville Lane-Fox, would not succeed. A local auctioneer with rooms in Vicar Lane conceived the idea of sending out Tory snatch squads sporting Liberal colours the night before the election to round up all the potential Liberal voters they could find who were in a state of intoxication. Owing to the amount of liquor readily available the task was easy and the haul substantial. The victims were taken to the Vicar Lane auction rooms and there, from a teapot, were plied with rum laced with laudanum, the idea being that the voters would either not get as far as the hustings or, if they did, might find that, being drunk, they would not be allowed by the returning officer to record their vote. On this particular occasion it was said that about 150 Liberal voters did not reach the hustings. This 'cooping' technique was locally known as 'teapotting'.

Public disturbance at election time was, of course, common. At the election of 1857 there were some doubts cast on Edward Auchmuty Glover's right to stand because of lack of appropriate property qualification. Philip C. Toker, a London lawyer who tried to expose Glover in Beverley, aroused the anger of the mob and, after initial sanctuary in the Lairgate office of the mayor Henry Silvester, Toker found refuge in the house of the Akrill family in the Market Place – initially in Miss Akrill's first-floor bedroom and later in the safer second-floor room of her mother. The mob lit a bonfire before the house but, thanks to heavy rain which had the dual effect of extinguishing the blaze and damping down enthusiasm, Toker was able to be spirited away through the Globe Inn yard to a welcome cab in Walkergate which took him through to Hull and safety. Glover was unseated on petition and the election which followed brought Henry Edwards into the political arena.

Electoral seduction was thereafter more extensive, intensive and sophisticated, pasture masters, charity trustees, the Working Men's Conservative Association, innkeepers, solicitors and town councillors alike being involved. Money was as furtively dispensed at the Mechanics Institute as at the Golden Ball. At the 1860 election 'the Man with the Hairy Cap' was busy paying voters £2 a man at the Pack Horse. Robert Walker's Gift (1854), designed to help poor freemen who lost animals, was even misused, for the pasture masters were all Edwards' men. For example, in expectation of a grant from the Gift, John Lancaster, a mechanic from Edwards' Iron and Waggon Works, bought an ailing horse on a Saturday (allegedly for £3): the animal died on the Sunday and he pocketed 15s. for the carcass on the Monday. Lancaster thereupon collected £3 from the pasture masters from Walker's Gift. But the dance had to end some time and, following a petition after the election of 1868 at which Anthony Trollope was a candidate, a Royal Commission was appointed to inquire into the electoral condition of Beverley, 757 witnesses being cross-examined and 45,709 questions asked. The report showed that wholesale corruption had been rife at all elections investigated between 1857 and 1868 and a schedule thereto (what might be termed the Beverley 'Black List') gives the names of 604 Beverlonians who were either bribers or who had been bribed during this period. As Richard Whiteing put it at the time, there were only three pure men in Beverley, Mr Hodgson the tanner, Mr Stephenson the brewer and himself – a dubious statement but one with which readers of Anthony Trollope's *Autobiography* and his *Ralph the Heir* (a novel published in 1871 and largely based on his Beverley experiences) would be inclined to agree.

But Beverley's lack of electoral purity must not obscure the fact that the Church – Anglican, Roman Catholic, Nonconformist – was flourishing. Victorian England, though assailed and disturbed by doubt, was both pious and religious, and church and chapel building, the increasing (if occasionally misguided) care for church fabrics, and a deepening concern with social problems are well manifest in Beverley. The Minster, during what might broadly be termed the Age of Canons Birtwhistle and Nolloth (1844-1921), saw the building of new chapels of ease in the two Minster parishes, St John's in Lairgate (1840) and Tickton (1844), as well as Woodmansey church school (1856 – followed by the consecration of a church there in 1898) and a chapel at Molescroft in 1896.

Services were improved and greater attention given to the cleanliness and beautification of the interior of the Minster. The 18th-century pulpitum screen of John Moyser's age – comical indeed to the Gothic Revivalists – was ousted and replaced (1876-81) by the present oak screen, designed by Gilbert Scott and executed by the Beverley master-craftsman

James Elwell. When Henry Edward Nolloth came up to Beverley from Chesham in 1880 to begin a 40-year ministry at the Minster, he inherited a programme of improvement initiated in the time of his predecessor, Canon John Birtwhistle, which undoubtedly inspired him to even greater endeavour. The Queen's Jubilee of 1897, for example, provided the occasion to launch a campaign to fill in the niches of the Minster's west front and towers – a programme of embellishment which did not go wholly uncriticised.

At St Mary's the story was similar if not so spectacular and the two Pugins and the two Scotts made their several contributions to fabric restoration and interior improvement. With all this was coupled social work of increasing earnestness. St Mary's Church House in Ladygate became a focal point of much practical endeavour and a centre from which the sick poor could be helped with meals, clothing and comforts. Temperance work was well to the fore in the town by the 1880s and, although the Coffee Tavern which Henry Nolloth opened in the Minster infants' schoolroom at Beckside in 1882 under the name of 'The British Workman', had by 1884 become a Cocoa House instead, the aims and objects were apparent from its official title.

St Nicholas church, 1879-80.

With the growth of population in the parish of St Nicholas, the demand for a new church began, stimulated after 1823 by interference with the old graveyard which had been let as a garden. In view of the union with St Mary's, rectorial enthusiasm was understandably lukewarm but in 1876 the building of what was, in effect, a memorial church to one of his sons was made possible as a result of a bequest by the first Baron Wolverton. Fortunately, another son was the Revd Edward Carr Glynn, vicar of St Mary's and rector of St Nicholas: otherwise the memorial church might well have been built in London's dockland. The new church, dedicated in 1880, was built somewhat to the north of the old St Nicholas church as on investigation the original site proved to be too wet.

The development of the other churches is just as noteworthy. Although the Roman Catholic community in the town was quite small, early in Victoria's reign numbers began to grow, helped later by Irish immigration. Shortly before the end of the century the present church of St John of Beverley, outside the North Bar, had already replaced an architecturally plainer building. The Congregationalists built a new and spacious church in Lairgate in 1887 – the fourth to occupy the site and, as the years passed, they felt the need for provision of a church in the more industrialised area of Grovehill. Dinner-hour services in the drawing loft of the shipyard there led in 1904 to the erection of a small iron church locally and affectionately known as 'the tin tabernacle'. In a 45-year ministry, unique in devotion, humility and pastoral care, the Revd Herbert Abba saw the pleasingly designed Latimer Memorial Church take its place in 1935.

Methodism in Beverley, on the other hand, reflected some of the problems of secession and misunderstanding which followed Wesley's death until unification of United, Wesleyan and Primitive Methodists was achieved in 1932. The Primitive Methodists, formed in 1811 after Hugh Bourne and William Clowes had been expelled from the Methodist church, became particularly strong in the Hull area and in 1825 built a chapel in Wednesday Market. In 1868 the chapel was replaced by a second, built on a larger scale, but 90 years later, with the congregation declining, this was demolished, the site ultimately being used for a garage.* Thereafter the Weslyan church in Toll Gavel, which had been opened in 1892, became the town's main Methodist church, smaller chapels serving other districts in the town. As has been noted, the Beverley Baptists had their respective chapels in Well Lane and in Swaby's Yard,† off Walkergate. In 1888 the Scotch Baptists of Walkergate built a new chapel in Morton Lane, now given up to secular use.‡ It was in 1881 that the Salvation Army, not exactly unhindered, began its religious and social work in Beverley and in 1884

---

* Crystal Garage was demolished to make way for Boyes store.
† Now Gingers Coffee Shop.
‡ Used by St John Ambulance Brigade.

Primitive Methodist Chapel, Wednesday Market, built 1868, now replaced by Boyes.

found it possible to begin the building of their Wilbert Lane Citadel, which was opened by General Booth in 1886.*

It is impossible to assess the extent of their social and charitable work but all these religious groups made an effective contribution in their several ways. Their various organisations, their mutual improvement societies and fellowships with their discussion and lecture programmes, following the pattern of the Mechanics Institute established in 1832 in Cross Street, played an important part in adult education. After this lapse of time one may be justified in questioning the educational value of a lecture given in 1858 under the title 'Frolics and caprices of fun and fancy', but at the same time there was the flavour of real earnestness about a discussion as to whether a burgess ought to sell his vote. The manifest enthusiasm for education and self-improvement helps to explain the movement in the 1880s for a university extension society in the town.

Church and chapel alike did much for primary education in Beverley and in consequence there was no necessity under the Education Act of 1870 to establish a school board in the town. The National schools of the Minster, St Mary's and St Nicholas, and the Wesleyan and Roman Catholic

---

* Demolished; replaced by Citadel Court 1997.

*Corn
Exchange,
1886, later the
Playhouse
Cinema.*

North Bar Within.

*North Bar
Without.*

Butcher Row.

Walkergate.

Walkergate: the great flood of 1912.

schools made adequate provision. In fact, a report of 1869 on the Foundation school (a fee-paying establishment for boys at the west end of Grayburn Lane, opened in 1861) commented on the fact that 'the elementary schools are so good that an excellent education is obtainable in them not only for the children of the labouring class but for those of the class immediately above them': the slightly superior class of child on the next rung of the ladder remained unspecified, but the class-conscious Victorian understood.

The Foundation school, together with the Blue Coat school, came to an end in 1890 when both were merged with the town's grammar school, and, following the Education Act of 1902, a grammar school for girls, or a high school as it was known, was established in Norwood in 1908. This public provision was interestingly reinforced by an increasing number of private school academies. Miss Downs' school in North Bar Without c.1860 was apparently offering a wide range of courses, from ancient history to French, music and 'use of the globes'. Nathaniel Blunsum in Minstermoorgate at the same time was taking boarders at 25 guineas a year and could publicly and somewhat airily testify to the fact that, in his establishment, 'deference was shown to the wants of the age', whatever that may have meant. Some of these schools were necessarily ephemeral and standards and quality to some extent are reflected in the anonymous advertisement in 1858 when two young ladies were sought for one such school: no salary was offered but, as the advertisement put it, 'improvement in their education will be sufficient remuneration for their services'.

★　★　★

Despite the reforms of 1835 town government did not progress as smoothly as the Whig reformers of the 1830's would have wished and, as in other boroughs, consideration of the problems of local government was frequently bedevilled by both faction and party squabbles. The town, for example, virtually escaped the great cholera epidemic of 1849 which ravaged Hull but, judging by council debate in 1850 which followed the report on the state of the town by G. T. Clark, superintending inspector to the General Board of Health, not all the lessons had been learned. Among others, the redoubtable Councillor Boyes, for example, saw no reason at all for waterworks and on the matter of waterborne sanitation eloquently expressed a conservative dislike for the water closet as such and a personal predilection for the traditional privy at the bottom of his garden. But improvement did come, more open sewers were culverted, lodging houses controlled, the cattle markets regulated and by-laws for sewerage and new streets laid down.

Further improvement came particularly in the 1880s. In 1881, not without objections from the Corporation and the local ratepayers' association, Parliamentary powers were obtained by the Beverley Waterworks Company to establish a waterworks, and building began the same year. A report on a virulent outbreak of typhoid fever in the town in 1884-85 stimulated action for a radical overhaul of the sewerage system, which was effected soon after 1888 with the building of the Beckside outfall works. Town improvement came in other ways too with the provision of other services and amenities. The Cottage Hospital, built on part of the site of the defunct Beverley Iron Works, was opened in 1886* and a scheme approved for its amalgamation with the old Beverley Dispensary which had been begun in 1823 by public subscription and with help from William Wilson's Charity. Thanks to the munificence of John Edward Champney, who provided the building, and the mayor, William Spencer, who gave the site, Beverley – earlier than many communities of its size – obtained a public library in 1906: books, however, were not issued to the public until stock had reached the level of 2,500 volumes the following year. In 1928 Champney, the bibliophile, provided a new wing to the original building: this housed the reference library, to which he donated his own valuable collection of books. In smaller ways, too, improvement came about as, for instance, by the planting of trees on the York, Walkington and Newbald roads in Westwood to mark the Queen's Jubilee.† In general from c.1880 the historian can discern the real beginnings of a continuing, conscious care for the urban environment.

Re-housing, and the demands of a population which by 1969 was over 17,000, has meant that within a restricted borough boundary building has been considerable, for geographically the existence of the pastures has prevented undue urban sprawl, especially to the west. The years between the two world wars marked the acquisition and the building over of the park land of the Hall in Lairgate. The post-1945 period witnessed extensive building north and east of the railway station as well as re-building in Wilbert Lane and elsewhere. In other ways and with lamentable lack of sympathy and understanding, the town at times has been sacrificed to the insatiable demands of the motor vehicle. In 1962 there was a vigorously contested official proposal to widen medieval Hengate for the benefit of through traffic, and the breaching of the Saturday Market Place at its northern end with the consequent partial obliteration of the old medieval street of Walkergate, in order to ease traffic flow, rightly excited widespread and justified criticism.

In 1965 the Council for British Archaeology considered that Beverley was one of 40 British towns 'so splendid and precious that the ultimate responsibility for them should be a national concern'. Despite the town's proximity to much-blitzed Hull, the Hitler war left Beverley virtually unscathed but the increasing volume of road traffic, without the taking of speedy measures to counter its worse effects, may well do in a decade what the wear of centuries has failed to bring about. It has been said officially

---

* Demolished 1992; replaced by Cottage Mews.
† The Diamond Jubilee, 1897.

that, as far as Beverley is concerned, the needs of traffic must take precedence over history and that 'History . . . cannot rate very high in the list of priorities'. An insensitivity to history is not an unusual phenomenon but those who would be associated with such attitudes – and they are not few – cannot complain if, in this day and age, they are ranked with vandals and numbered among the Philistines. The purpose of this short history, with all its shortcomings and omissions, has been to try to set forth some record of Beverley through the centuries – that is the lesson of the past for the guidance of the present, and what the Beverley of the future is to be is very much the responsibility of the present.

Ladygate, showing the Globe Inn, later demolished for the building of Sow Hill Road.

Beverley Beck, with new housing.

Select Bibliography of Books published since 1972

Beverley Minster. ed. Rosemary Horrox (Beverley 2000)
Brown, Philip, *Old Beverley* (East Yorkshire Local History Society 1983)
Brown, Philip, *Philip Brown's Beverley* (Hull 1989)
Crowther, Jan, *Beverley in Mid-Victorian Times* (Cherry Burton 1990)
Deans, Patricia E. and Markham, John, *Beverley* (Stroud 1995)
Diary of a Yorkshire Gentleman, The ed. Susan and David Neave (Otley 2001)
Hall, Ivan and Elisabeth, *Historic Beverley* (York 1973)
History of the County of York, East Riding, Vol VI, ed. K. J. Allison (Oxford 1989)
Hopkins, Pamela, *The History of Beverley, East Yorkshire* (Pickering 2003)
Kirby, R. Martyn, *Sanctuary. Beverley – A Town of Refuge* (Beverley 1982).
Miller, Keith; Robinson, John; English, Barbara and Hall, Ivan. *Beverley, An Archaeological and Architectural Study* (HMSO 1982)
Pevsner, Nikolaus and Neave, David, *Yorkshire: York and the East Riding* (1995)
Sherwood, David, *Complete Streets of Beverley* (Beverley 2002).

INDEX

40; granted income from former estates, 39-40; sanctuary, 5, 40-1; inventory of vestments and valuables (1553), 41; new chapels of ease (1840-96), 81
Minster: clergy, 20-2, 27; appointed by Corporation, 65, incumbents, 65-6
Minster: fabric: frithstool (*frithstol*), 3, 4, 26; pulpitum, gift of Archbishop Ealdred, 7-8; damage by fire (1188), 22-3; collapse of tower (1213), 23; rebuilding 23-7; Percy tomb, 26; choir stalls and misericords, 26-7; Percy Chapel, 34; chapter house and charnel house demolished (1550), 39; repairs (1714-19), 62-3; addition of cupola (1721), 63; organ installed, 64; Victorian refurbishments, 81-2
Minster (New) Vicarage, 54
Minster (Old) Vicarage, 52
Minster Yard North, 52
Minstermoorgate, 6, 50, 54, 70, 87
Mitchell, Thomas, first vicar of Minster, 38, 41-2
Molescroft, 47, 81
Monasterboice (Co. Louth), monastery of, 2
Monasteries, dissolution of the, 35-41
Morality plays *see* Gild plays
Morant, Wynand, merchant, 10
Mountain, Charles the Younger, Hull architect, designs extensions to Guildhall, 50
Moyser, James, designs Ann Routh's Hospital, 54,
Moyser, John, and repairs to Minster, 63
Mudfysch, John, supplier of bricks for North Bar, 15
Mynskip, Edward, 49
National Schools, 70, 84
Nelson, Marmaduke, alderman, 69
Neville, Alexander, archbishop of York, 17, 22, 25
New Walk, 52, 56, 58; constructed, 60
Newbald Road, 88
Newbegin, 53
Newbegin Bar, *14*, 15, 52; demolished (1790), 60
Nolloth, Canon Henry Edward, Minster, 26, 81-2
Norris, John, schoolmaster, 69
North Bar, *14*, 15, 52, 59, *85*
North Bar Within (North Bar Street), *13*, 45, 56, 58, 70, *85*
North Bar Without, 83, *85*, 87
Norwood, 56, 61
Norwood Bar, 15

Norwood House, 56
Ogle, Oswin, son-in-law of Sir Ralph Ellerker q.v., 35
Packer, John, merchant, of Hull, 39
Parliamentary elections, 70-1; disenfranchisement for corruption, 80-1
Pasture Masters, 79-80
Pastures, 6, 16-17, 78-80
Pearson, Nicholas, schoolmaster, parish clerk and diarist, 47
Peesgrave, John, fuller and heretic, 42
Pelham (family), Earls of Yarborough, 70; and Beverley Parks estate, 52
Pennyman, Sir James, MP, builds Lairgate Hall, 54
Percy (family), 33-4
Percy, Eleanor, wife of Henry, 1st Lord Percy of Alnwick, 26
Percy, Henry, 4th Earl of Northumberland, murdered 1489, 25
Percy, Henry, 4th Lord Percy of Alnwick, defeated at Bramham Moor (1408), 15
Percy, Idonea, wife of Henry, 2nd Lord Percy of Alnwick, 26
Pighill Lane, *see* Manor Road
Pilgrimage of Grace, 33, 35, 36-7, 42
Pont l'Evêque, Roger de, archbishop of York, provost of Beverley, 21
Pope, John, of London, purchases friary lands, 37
Population, 33, 39, 44, 73, 88
Pottage, town councillor, 79
Prattman, John, builder, extends Ann Routh's Hospital, 55
Primitive Methodists, 68, 83, *84*
Public health, 18, 44-5, 59, 87-8
Public Library, 88
Puch, thegn, 2
Quakers, 69
Railway, opened, 73-4; extension to York, and further planned extensions, 74; station, *72*, 88
Railway Street, 74
Regal Cinema, 56
Rickman, Thomas, 64
Rigby, Revd Robert, St Mary's, 66
Rise, Roger de, first vicar of St Mary's, 27
Robinson, James Mowld, town councillor, 74
Robinson, Mark, Church Methodist, 68
Rokeby, Sir Richard, benefactor of St Mary's, 35
Roman Catholics, 41-2, 83
Rooland, Thomas, prior of Warter, 32
Routh, Ann, hospital of, 53, 54

Rumbald, Samson Augustus, 71
Rushforth, Edward, designs obelisk for
  Wednesday Market, 49
Russell, Simon, 29
St Elena's chapel, 31
St Giles' hospital, 32
St Giles Croft, 32
St John of Beverley, bishop of Hexham,
  bishop of York, 2, 4, 7, 24-5; tomb
  of, *3*
St John's chapel, Lairgate, 68
St John's hospital, Lairgate, 32
St Mary Magdalene's hospital,
  Killingwoldgraves, 39
St Mary's church, *28*; origins of, 27-9;
  inventory of vestments and valuables
  (1553), 41; parish united with St
  Nicholas, 62; income 64-5
St Mary's church: clergy, incumbents, 66
St Mary's church: fabric, collapse of tower
  (1520), 35; modernising work, 64;
  Victorian refurbishments, 82
St Mary's Church House, 82
St Mary's Court, *13*
St Mary's hospital, 32
St Mary's Manor, building of, 59
St Michael's church, Cherry Burton,
  origins of, 2
St Nicholas' church, 29-30; inventory of
  vestments and valuables (1553), 41; out
  of use during 17th century, 62; rebuilt
  1880, *82*, 83
St Nicholas' hospital, 30
St Thomas' chapel, 29
Salvation Army, 83-4
Sandholme, 16
Sandwith, Miss, her school, North Bar
  Within, 70
Saturday Market, 16, *46*, 49, 77, 80, *85*, 88
Sawney, manufacturer of agricultural
  implements, 75, 77
Scarborough, William, vicar of St Mary's,
  contributor to building of North Bar, 15
Schools, 39, 40, 54, 69-70, 84, 87
Scotch Baptists, 83
Sessions House, *67*; building of, 56-7
Shelton, Samuel, of Wakefield, designs
  Market Cross, 49
Shipyard, 75, *76*
Shout, William, surveys Minster fabric, 64
Simpson, William, tanner, 74
Snetzler, John, builder of Minster organ, 64
South Bar *see* Keldgate Bar
Sow Hill Road, *89*
Spencer, William, mayor, 88

Spendlove, Henry, new house in Hengate,
  53
Sperrin, William, political commentator, 71
Springs, 9
Stanhope, Michael, buys and demolishes
  many church buildings, c.1547, 38-9
Stapleton, Elizabeth, mother of William
  q.v., 36
Stapleton, William, of Wighill, rebel, 36
Station Square, 75
Stephenson, Robert and Son, brewers, 77
Stork, 16
Streets, 59, 60, 87; Scandinavian elements
  in names of, 6; *see also* under names of
  individual streets
Strickland, William, reluctant alderman, 71
Sumner, Gillyat, 79
Swaby's Yard, 69, 83
Swinemoor, 16
Tanning industry, 74-5
Taylor, John, of Molescroft, Royalist, 47
Temperance movement, 82
Thackray, Mr, linen draper, 52
Thomas of Bayeux, archbishop of York, 21
Thomas the Younger, provost of Beverley,
  21
Thompson, William, joiner, makes chairs
  for Guildhall, 50
Thorne, 61
Thornton, John de, merchant, 11
Thornton, William, work on Hotham's
  Beverley house, 53; repairs to Minster,
  63
Thorold, priest of St Nicholas, 29
Tickton, 81
Tigar, Pennock, colour manufacturer, 73, 75
Todd, Edward, 60
Toker, Philip C., 80-1
Toll Gavel, 60, 68, 70, 83
Tonge (pasture), 16, 49
Town ditch, archaeological investigation of,
  1
Trinities, moated site of the Hospitallers,
  31, 45
Trinity Hospital, 32
Trinity Lane, 31
Trollope, Anthony, novelist and failed
  parliamentary candidate, 59, 81
Trollope, Richard, alderman of painters'
  gild, fined for poor quality of play, 12
Turner, Matthew, printer, 77
Tymperon's Almshouses, 54
Valiant Soldier, public house, Norwood, 61
Valloines, Sybil de, benefactor of Kinghts
  Hospitaller, 31

Vicar Lane, 80
Walker, Admiral Francis, owner of Lairgate Hall, 54
Walker Beck, 9, 11, 18
Walkergate, 6, 32, 54, 61, 67, 68, 70, 83, 86, 88
Walkington Road, 88
Waltham, William de, canon of Beverley and York, 25
Warter, William de, merchant, 10
Warter Priory, 32
Warton (family), 47, 48, 70
Warton, Charles, hospital of, Minstermoorgate, 54
Warton, Sir Michael, MP, 37; helps to rebuild Market Cross, 49; house, 59; appeals for funds to repair Minster, 62-3; leaves money to Minster, 63-4
Warton, Warton, new house in Newbegin, 53
Watson, Charles, architect, of York, designs Sessions House, 56
Watts, John, carrier, 77
Wednesday Market, 45, 49, 60, 68, 83, 84
Well Lane, 66, 69, 83
Wesley, John, 68
Wesleyan Methodists, 83
Wesleyan school, 84
Westwood, 16, 17, 78
Wetadun, nunnery of, identification with Watton, 2
Whincop, Revd Thomas, Minster, 65
White Horse, public house, Hengate, 56, 62
Whitefield, George, Methodist preacher, 68
Whiteing, Richard, 37-8, 81
Wickwane, William, archbishop of York, 16, 49
Wilbert Lane, 84, 88
Wilkinson, Tate, theatre impresario, 48
Williamson, Luke, 52
Wilson, Richard, rebel, 37
Winter, Thomas, provost of Beverley, 21
Witty, Charles, 55
Wolfkeld, 18
Wolsey, Cardinal Thomas, archbishop of York, 34
Wood, William, miller, 79
Wood Lane, 32, 68, 69
Woodmansey, 81
Woodmansey, William, rebel, 37
Workhouse, Minstermoorgate, 50
Wressle, 34
Wrightson, Richard, abuser of councillors (1604), 44
Wrightson, Thomas, builder, develops

Hotham Beverley estate, 53, builds Ann Routh's Hospital, 54
Wrightson, William, builder, builds Newbegin Bar House (1745), 52
Wygthon, Henry, donor of land to Franciscan friary, 31
Yarborough, Earls of, Beverley Parks estate, 37, 52
York Road, 88